The Correct Decision

Freedom Versus Evil And Ignorance

By

Jamil Kazoun

(Jamil Talaat Malak Sukkarieh Kazoun)

Previously titled: The Man That Shot The Law

Version 2.02

ISBN-13: 9798692091703

Library of Congress Control Number: 2022903917

Subject: Civics, politics, law, mathematics, decision theory, statistics

September 21, 2019

Table of Contents

The Town Of FO 6

Which Way Do I Go? 25

The Index Of Social Intelligence: 68

Some notes follows: 81

    For A Book To Teach Children Important Math Concepts 106

    A Mental Experiment In Guessing: Humans Versus Coin Machines 112

    Degree Of Freedom 118

    Academic Future Project For Increasing Human Intelligence 125

    A Vote Result Calculator Example: 130

This Book Is About Freedom 144

The Town Of FO

How Oppression Started

A short story

A family was living alone in a remote area, on a private piece of land that they farmed, grew chicken, and where their children played.

There was no school. The parents taught the children as they pleased. And the children helped in daily chores.

No one could tell them what to do.

They were far from other towns and cities.

They had no laws or regulations to live under.

They lived in freedom as they pleased, and had peace.

They farmed the land and became successful and able to provide for their needs.

They made and sold their products at nearest markets as they pleased, without any interference.

They hired and fired help as needed, as they pleased, and paid them wages as both sides agreed. No one interfered.

They washed their clothes, swam, and bathed nude in the nearby river.

They celebrated with music, dance, alcohol, and the pipe, as they pleased and when they pleased.

That was their life.

Then suddenly, strangers, about nine families, poor, uneducated, heard of this rural area, and how nice it is, and decided to move there to live.

In few days, they build poor shacks from wood and leaves, and made them their homes.

In few days, a large area that had only one family there, now had ten families.

One person among these new people, heard, or read, or was told, or thought: It would be wise to change this informal rural isolated area, into a formal town.

So he gathered the nine new families in a meeting and they agreed. They declared the area a town, and elected this idea man as its mayor.

A new town was born.

The town was given the name of F.O. and became known as The Town Of FO.

The next day the mayor held a town meeting and said:

We need a constitution of law to govern this town. I suggest a simple one:

We can decide any matter and make it binding on all if we put the issue to a vote and 51% or more agree.

The attendants agreed on this as their constitution.

The next day, they held a town meeting and decided on the laws that would govern them.

The mayor said: It would be good to have a salary and office for me and staff as essential for government function. They agreed.

Another said: I have no money to educate my children. But it is important that they get an education.

The town of FO should build a school and ensure the students have mandatory attendance.

Another said: I think we should ban alcohol and smoking because I don't drink or smoke and I know they are bad for health.

Another said: Pork is against my religion.

It should be banned, its sale and use.

Another said: Nudity is a shame.

I saw a poor man outside who had no clothes on him.

We must not allow it.

Is that not against religions or morality?

A young man questioned: Would this apply to children also? What about in private?

I ask because I have little children, boys, that run around the house nude.

Would these be legal or illegal acts by my children?

I and my 17 years old child also walk nude in the house. Are we allowed this as adults?

And by the way, if we allowed nudity only in private, does it mean we are allowed other banned things as long as done in private?

And what about women?

Will they also be under this new law.

I am thinking it might be very good for us men to be able to see women nude on the street.

The discussion went on for a long while, and it was very tense.

Men seemed to be worried about being seen nude, or seeing other men nude.

Women had similar concerns.

It was as if much human law was written simply to cover men's and women's physical insecurities.

Men's aggression against men

and against women.

And women's aggressive attitudes,

and the need for control by law

seemed as if it was wrapped up in the psychology of public nudity.

The majority wanted control of this issue.

Another said: We should look at the vegetables people sell,

to see if their shape and size are acceptable.

I had heard somewhere that in some far-off lands, called the EU countries, they had banned the sale of some vegetables based on shape or size.

Now that I heard this, I think they may be right,

and it is starting to offend my senses too, to see a cucumber or carrot that is not straight,

or a kiwi fruit that is too small.

The issue was not discussed much and was agreed upon. They had reasoned these far-off countries are very rich,

and advanced in technology,

and we may be wise to imitate them.

Another said: I don't have a job,

but if I get one, it should guarantee health insurance, my retirement, and be strictly regulated to ensure my safety and happiness.

I have asthma, and the air should be filtered there. Are we not entitled to clean air?

I would like to sue an employer that does not provide me this.

They looked at each other and said:

Of course!

Who could be against clean air.

Clean air is essential for good health. What could be more basic than that?

Are employers trying to hurt us if they do not comply?

I am sure doctors also would not be happy if employers did not do it.

Who wants such cruelty to the people that serve them?

One of them stood up and asked: Are these to be regulations on farms also?

I had heard that cows' farts generate lots of methane,

and I wonder if we should require farm owners to use carbon filter masks on cows' buttocks.

A child in the town hall meeting stood up and said: I love strawberry ice-cream,

can we pass a law for that,

please?

Touched by the politeness and sweetness of this little child,

and by the love the neighbours had for him,

they collectively said "sure we can, and we will!"

But the mayor suddenly said "No" to the child.

Silence fell on the meeting

as residents started to wonder if they had elected a heartless man to office,

a mayor that is unresponsive to the demands of citizens.

Others had the flash idea occur to them of how to remove this newly elected mayor from office. We had just elected him.

But then, the mayor continued to speak saying:

You are entitled to have strawberry ice-cream,

but we do not need to make it a law.

Since we have made the creation of a public school mandatory,

and since attending school is mandatory,

and since these schools have a mandate to create their own mandates,

we can put this as a rule of the school system mandates,

that strawberry ice-cream is available to students daily.

A big sigh of relief came over the attending residents as they saw the love, care, and especially the logical capabilities of their new mayor in solving problems.

An older man with no teeth stood up and warned the child "but be careful about eating too much ice-cream because it may rut your teeth. Look at me.

Look at what happened to my teeth from eating too many sweets. No teeth.

I propose the rule to limit child consumption of ice-cream to two cones daily. And by the way, can we pass a law to provide free dentures for the elderly only.

Young people with missing teeth should be able to handle this problem, but for the elderly, it is a big problem".

The logic and arguments presented by these citizens were too powerful for most, and they approved these two issues together in one vote.

Two friends were sitting next to each other, and one whispered to the other "Do you believe this? Why did we not think of this before?" His friend asked "What?"

He replied "I cannot believe how stupid we are. This may be too easy. You and I planned to steal some of the animals in the old farmhouse.

Let us try this, propose a law to get their animals or their money, so we can get some food to eat." His friend rose up and said "I propose that no human being should go without food to eat. To not have food is inhuman, it is heartless, not kind. A human being should be entitled to a minimum amount of food, and especially the children and the pregnant." His friend whispered back "That's pretty good. I especially like this 'entitled' word you used."

And with hardly a minute passing of discussion time, they all shouted approval, and the proposed law was adopted.

Another child who had just learned the multiplication table rose up to say: The multiplication table is 100% correct and is the truth. And, it is extremely useful.

I think it should be a requirement to use it as a law.

Another adult, his aunt,

rose up in full admiration of such knowledge and wisdom displayed by this child.

And almost in tears, she declared support for this,

which moved the citizens to immediately approve it as a law.

The citizens kept on like this all night, giving each other rights or restrictions as they pleased, enacting laws that to them seemed logical, because they knew in their heart these are good laws by good people for good people.

They were also motivated and drunk by a new motto they created: "Equality and fairness for all. Love to mankind. We are all the same, and deserve good things".

They set all these as their rights that should not be violated, else the violator would be prosecuted.

The next day, they met again.

It dawned on them that all these laws and demands require money. They had no money.

So they passed a new law that said: The community has needs. Those who have money are obligated to provide for our needs.

They called this law The Taxation Law. And it specified that: If you do not pay what we think is a fair amount to pay, you will be imprisoned.

We can take your existing and future property until you pay your assessed taxes.

They created an office, called Taxation Office, and made its insignia a gun, to always remind citizens of the power of this office.

To determine how much each citizen should pay in taxes, they made what to them seemed like a logical decision: Whatever the government total expenses are, that is the total to be paid by citizens.

They wrote specifically saying: We, the government, are giving the people many things. Should they not pay for it? How can you not understand this?????

They had intentionally added five question marks to the end of this sentence and question for emphasis.

These questions seem to have been written down so that this office will always know how important it is to the government, and how rightful this office is in its assigned duty.

These questions seemed to have been written as if from fear, that without such money, the government cannot exist.

If this office disappeared, the entire government could disappear with it.

Since these residents were poor with no money, except for the single family that originally was living here, they decided that those with little or no money should not pay taxes, because "it is not fair to ask money from the poor.

And that those who have money should bear the total cost."

Since there was only one family in town that may have money, one family out of ten families, representing 10% of the households, it was decided that the 10% of the households will pay all government cost.

The logic to them was clear: WE want these services and benefits, and, THEY have money, and should pay for them.

The next day, the government waited on the Taxation Office to bring revenues. The Taxation Office sent its men out to collect taxes.

Having calculated who can pay and how much, they went to the original family of the area. This family had been absent from their home for few months.

They had their parents in the emergency room in a distant hospital, and left to be with them.

Having come back to their home, and not aware of all the things that quickly happened in their absence, without their knowledge or consent, they heard a knock at the door of their house.

At the door, the government taxation officials introduced themselves.

They showed their official badge, with the department's gun symbol on it.

And told them: You have been assessed tax obligation of this amount of money.

You must pay it now, or you will be arrested and imprisoned, and your house and property taken under our control until sold, and

you will be shamed in public as tax evaders and deadbeats with your name placed on public boards.

We will confiscate your passport and travel rights, so you cannot escape.

If you do not pay now, get dressed and come with us without resistance.

We are merciless as the kings and lords' men of the past collecting taxes, taking chicken or property or killing on the spot.

This wealth is not yours anymore.

It belongs to the community, your neighbours, because your neighbours enacted laws allowing the taking of your money.

Sir, I see you have chicken. Do you think your neighbours don't like to eat chicken? How do you expect them to live if they do not get some of your chicken to eat?

The man of the house was listening as if he was in a dream.

He wondered if this was a nightmare dream.

He wondered: who are these men before me?

What is a tax department and this town government they are talking about.

We did not have them few months ago.

When was it created? Who did it? What does it do? What does my family have to do with it?

We neither know what it is nor asked for anything from it? How can they come barging into our home like this?

He looked around him as if double checking if this is real or surreal.

Then he told the officials:

I don't know who you are and what you do and who gave you authority to come here like this.

We have aggressed against no one, for anyone to interfere in our life.

We asked for no services from you to owe you money for.

We have no money to pay, nor do we want to pay you.

Go away.

The officials immediately surrounded him, and forced him to come with them, putting him under arrest, as a violator of the law, and thus, as a criminal.

On the way to prison, he was informed of additional charges the town had brought against him.

That he will get an extra year of jail for failing to change his house colour to red, as the town newly required of all households.

They had passed a law for this because red was a symbol of love, and they wanted everyone to remember this and live by it in their community.

The man could not comprehend all these charges, and laws that he was arrested under, and was unable to defend himself against them and their logic. So, he was put immediately in jail for years.

That night of arrest, his wife and children prayed together saying:

We were living in peace and freedom all our lives until these strangers, do-gooders, loving and caring people, came to live nearby.

Now, so quickly, look at what is happening.

We pray that one of these options will happen:

1. A good size meteor strikes these people at the right spot, but let it happen when we are away from the town, or

2. A virus attacks and kills them all, or great percentage of them, or

3. They get struck by a disease that leaves them unable to speak all their lives.

And the family kept on going like this for few minutes,

giving their god options,

so that maybe he can make one of these options come true.

And when they stopped their options listing, the family together concluded the prayer saying:

Amen.

After one year of the father's continued imprisonment, one of his sons decided to do something about the sad situation of his family. He thought that if life soured because of the nine families that moved into the area, and their creation of a simple majority rule government, then maybe he should try to do the same to them. So, he decided to divide the large parcel of land the family owned into small pieces, and to give these pieces to the large number of relatives they had living in nearest towns. He acted on this and gave these lands for free on condition they will move in to live there, even offering help building houses or shacks. About 20 families from his relatives accepted the offer, and quickly moved in to build houses and live there.

He gathered them in a meeting, and told them what had happened to his family and of his plan to take over the town, as these strangers did before. The relatives were glad to help and offered complete support. At the next town meeting, it was election time. The son nominated himself for mayor, and easily won as he expected.

The next day the new mayor held his first public meeting. He had previously come to know that the previous mayor hated the colour blue, and that the town people hated dancing, because they thought of themselves as pious, and they loved taxation because it brought them benefits.

The new mayor proposed needed changes, and said every town house is required to be painted blue as a community standard.

They discussed the proposed law.

Some said, that this is an imposition and it will cost them money to do, money they may not have, or need for other purposes.

Others said "Sure, but let us increase taxes on those able to pay for this".

There were many ideas.

The previous mayor sitting in the meeting looked extremely displeased, but said nothing.

They voted and the law was adopted easily by a majority as expected.

Next, the mayor proposed that taxes should be based on how much you like them. The more you like taxes, the higher your taxes will be. He told them, "Your happiness is important, and taxes seem to make many of you happy. And those who do not like taxes, do not have to pay any. All services will be paid for on service bases. But those who want taxes will be obliged to pay taxes, based on percentage of how much they like taxes."

The mayor asked for a show of hands asking "how many of you want 75% taxation level?" and they took the names of these people, and he asked "how many want 50% level?" and he kept on like this asking to the zero level, and recorded the names accordingly. He asked that this would be the law.

A discussion followed, and many seemed absolutely stunned by this new law.

Some said "sure, we love taxation, but not on us".

Others said "We are so poor; how can you force taxation on us. That is heartless. You are so unkind". The mayor answered "No one is forcing taxation on you. You said you want taxation and at a high level, and that is what you will get." One man angrily replied "Yes I want taxation and high taxation, but not on me. I am poor".

Another said "taxation is a community right, I am poor now and you are not, but what if you become poor in the future, don't you want something you can fall back on?"

The new mayor had reasoned that this was the idea of communal responsibility, an alternative to individual responsibility of taking care of yourself now, and save for hard times and the future. It was the core of the matter, individual freedom of choice and individual responsibility versus no freedom of choice and forced social responsibility. "No freedom" because a person had no choice whether to pay taxes or not, and "forced social responsibility" because you are being forced to be responsible for others whether you want to or not. It was a central issue in the freedom debate. Freedom or no freedom. There seemed to be no middle ground with freedom, you either have it complete or you do not. And incomplete freedom seemed to be just that, incomplete. An incomplete freedom can equal the complete taking of someone's freedom. You may care less about your freedom of choice and sell it for a dollar or a meal, and your concern is only about your needs, without care how you get them, be it robbing, lying, or force of law, but others, even when hungry, may spill their blood or donate their life for freedom of choice. There seems to be no calculator for freedom's cost.

Others cussed at the new mayor, calling him names. But he was unmoved, and he knew he had the support he needed to pass the law.

The discussion ended, they voted, and the new law was adopted as expected. The murmuring and cussing continued for a while.

A girl sitting in the audience asked the mayor "will serving free strawberry ice-cream in my school be affected by all this?"

The mayor said he did not know. And he told her to consider having her parents donate this to her school or to her, or seek a private effort to make it available, if this was very important to her.

That concluded the new mayor's first day.

The next day, at the town hall meeting, the old mayor rose up and declared publicly: "I refuse to paint my house blue."

The mayor told him "you are therefore breaking our laws. This is unwise. It carries a 1-year jail sentence." He added, it is important to obey the law, and I propose a new law that "those who publicly declare they will not obey the law, have to dance for two hours in front of the public hall." And he asked for discussion and a vote on this.

During the discussion, one man asked the mayor "Are you crazy? Forcing people to dance as punishment?"

The old mayor, full of anger, added "do you mind explaining your reasoning for this law?"

The mayor answered "mob rule."

The old mayor said "I do not understand."

The mayor said "mob rule. It is when there is more of one group than another, and this bigger group out win them, by force of guns, intimidation, or sheer numbers, deception, etc."

He added, "You see this group over there", motioning with his hand, "they are all my supporters. Whatever I propose, they will support, and they are a majority here."

A man commented "you mean there is no logic to your laws?"

The mayor replied "there is, and I just told you. It is mob rule. This is the logic."

Some started to snicker, some started to laugh. One said "that is an interesting new logic."

The mayor said "it is not new logic; it is common logic. I did a survey of law-making practices. This is almost uniformly the logic used."

One woman replied "How can that be? How can you do this to us?"

The mayor replied "You did this to my family before. You arbitrarily gave yourself power to rule over us, and forced us to comply with your rules. What do you call that?"

A man replied "Democracy. Majority rule."

The mayor said "Majority rule is just what it says. If there is a majority, they can force others to do their wishes. Is this proper?"

There was quiet for a while, as some started to think about what is being said.

After a while, a man said in frustration "freedom or no freedom. This is all talk. We need laws and we want government. How can you operate a government and laws without majority rule?"

The mayor replied "Neither I, nor my family want or asked for your laws or government. I became mayor out of necessity. I aim to dismantle this government and its laws."

The man replied "This is so stupid. I am going to see what I can do about this".

The mayor said "You do not seem to understand the situation, and you called my actions stupid. Let me illustrate" and he added "I now call on the assembly to consider this law: Anyone that uses the word 'stupid' to describe the mayor's action will have a mandatory 1-year imprisonment, and a monetary fine."

Immediately, they began consideration of the new proposal. After a set time of discussion, they voted, and the law was adopted.

The old mayor rose up and said "There is no freedom in this town, there is no freedom even for speech. I am going to raise this issue to our supreme court. To overrule you."

The mayor seemed puzzled and asked what is a supreme court?

The seemingly learned old mayor answered "How can you not know about the court system, and especially the supreme court?" He laughed and said "A man in your position, and not know this?"

The mayor asked "Do they also have a mob system between them? Or a mob system on others? Or both?"

The new mayor spoke "I want you to understand". He asked for consideration of a new law, and he said, "I propose the rape of any woman you see or like". The people present were stunned. Many shouted opposition to such law. Even his supporters. His supporters looked at each other, puzzled, as if they were asking "what do we do now?" But they trusted this person, and personally knew him extremely well, that the question in their minds became "why is he proposing this law?" they said to themselves "there must be good reason. Let us see". And they raised their hands in support of the new law. And the new law was adopted.

The old mayor asked himself out loud as if in disbelief letting all hear "how can this happen? How can this man be here? In this position? Making all these laws? All these impositions on us? I cannot believe this."

And then, as if he heard himself, and as if others heard him, and remembered how things were when they first came to town, created the government and created the laws, paused in silence.

The pause was very long.

The mayor in his seat also in silence, just looked at them, with arms open and outstretched towards them, and turning his head side to side to look at them individually, kept silence.

The few standing persons in the room, ready to speak, sat down. The silence was complete and long.

The old mayor, as if he had been awakened from a bad nightmare, rose up, dishevelled, as if hit by a car, as if broken, as if he was told his son was jailed or his dad lost his life. As if he had just stepped by accident on an innocent baby and killed him. He seemed in tremendous distress. He rose up, and as if he could not maintain his stand, very slowly sat down again.

He started looking around the room at the attendants. Not saying one word. The silence was broken with one man shouting "we are not stupid. We may have done some mistakes... But we are not stupid."

Another said "maybe we did not know what we were doing. But we meant well."

Another looked at the old mayor and requested "Please say something."

But the old mayor seemed dazed, realizing the calamity he had caused the family of the new mayor. Little was known about the background of the old mayor, his education, or his experience. But he seemed struck by a very deep realization.

Barely able to speak, he told the mayor "I am very sorry. Very sorry about what happened." He tried to get up, but as if he aged 50 years in one second, struggled, and some rushed to help him. He spoke softly and barely audible "no harm was intended," and repeated it while turning his back to leave the hall. "I am not feeling well now, I must leave" he said.

After several minutes of silence, the mayor said "tomorrow, I intend to close the government permanently. All services will be given to the employees to use as pay per service private companies. And I will set a final law that says: "In this town, it is illegal to make laws. Anyone attempting this may be punished by any local citizen at will. We do not accept that a man rules over another by force of gun, or force of law.”

Which Way Do I Go?

Suppose you were driving a car and came to a fork in the road — one road to the left and one road to the right — and only one of these two roads would take you to your destination, and you did not know which road to take. Now, assume that there are one hundred law-makers standing at the fork of the road, and they decide to help you find your way to your destination. So you ask them: Which way do I go? Left or right? Two options. And fifty percent of the law-makers decide you should go right, and fifty percent decide you should go left.

The information they provided has zero value because the number of people telling you to go left equals the number of people telling you to go right, and this gives us no guidance at all. Zero guidance on how to proceed. It would be like tossing a coin to decide. Your decision would be based on 50-to-50 percent chance of luck and not based on intelligence. The number telling you to go left equals and cancels the number telling you to go right. If the total number of people involved were 2, 100, or one million, as long as fifty percent say go one way, and the other fifty percent say go the other way, the numbers cancel each other and their collective advice has no value because you cannot confidently choose based on their advice. The confidence in your choice will be low, minimum, and your risk is high, maximum. The confidence or certainty will be 0% and the risk will be 100%. The information value of this vote is zero. The vote gives no guidance as to how to proceed, Left or Right. Any other result is better because it tells you which group is likely more correct, where a 90% to 10% result says the YES group is more likely correct and a 10% to 90% says the NO group is more likely correct. But at 50% to 50% the certainty or confidence level on how to proceed is minimal. Look at the graphs:

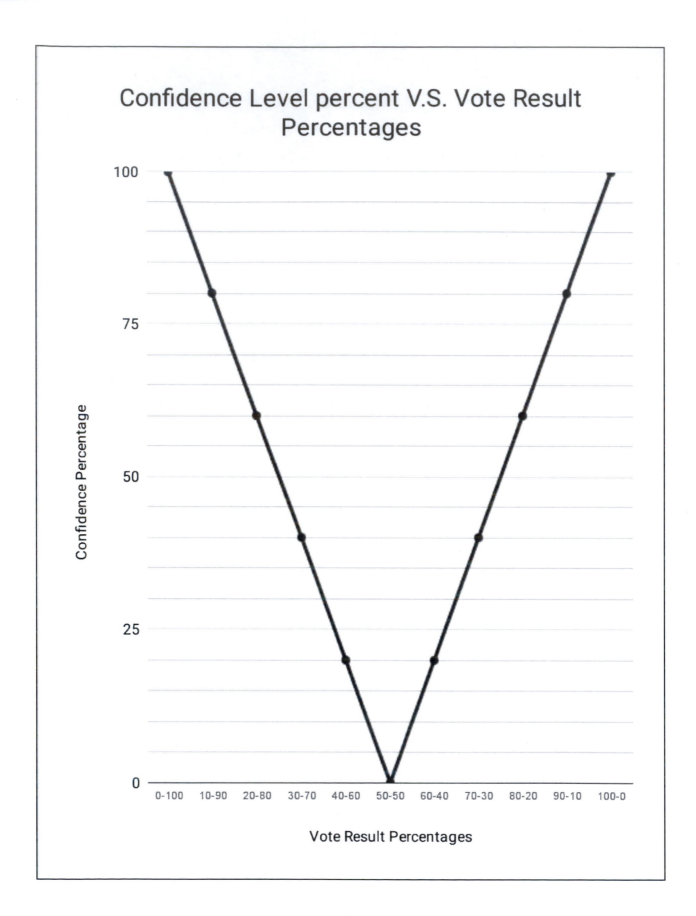

Confidence Level percent V.S. Vote Result Percentages

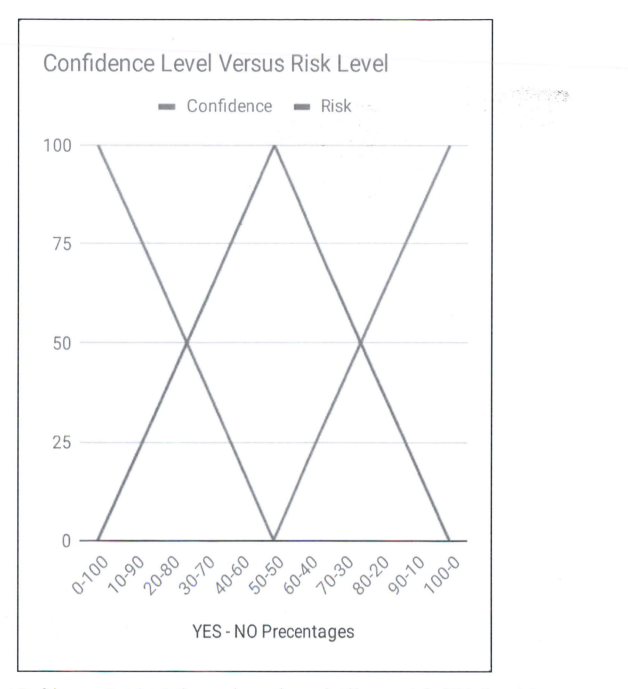

Note that Confidence or Certainty is the complement (somewhat like opposite) of Risk. If one is low the other is high. If confidence level is low, risk level is high. If confidence level is high, risk level is low. Risk = 100% minus Confidence. Example: For a 50% YES to 50% NO vote: Confidence = 0%, because 50% chance Left minus 50% chance right = 0% confidence whether to choose Left or Right. Also at that point, the Risk = 100%, (from the formula 100% minus 0% = 100%). For voting in a congress, parliament, city hall, or a court, the focus typically starts at vote result of 50% to 50% and above. So let me erase the not needed part of these graphs.

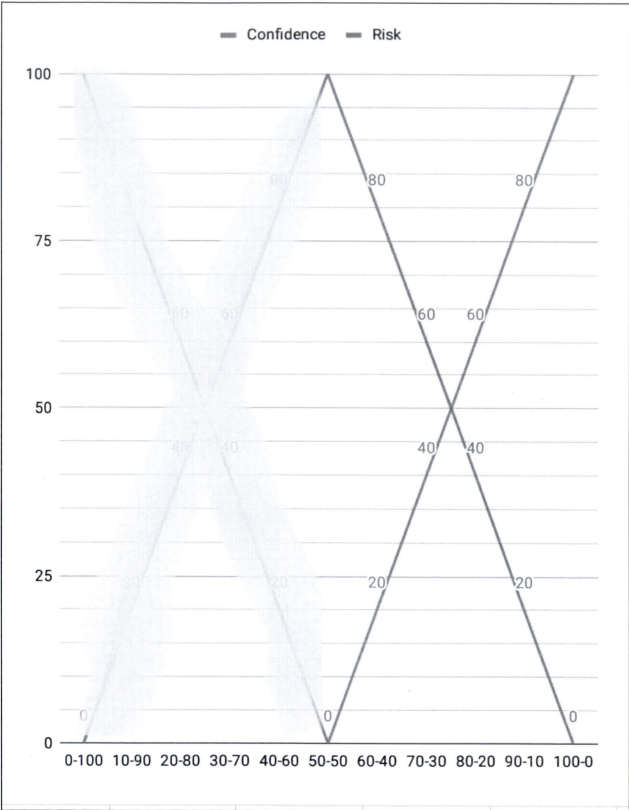

Mathematical Distraction: You can completely ignore this paragraph, but I add it for mathematicians to know that while the writings in this book are for the casual reader, the underlying mathematics formulas are standard. So in the mathematics of probability, the voters are called "the sample", and for choosing one side of the available options YES or NO, to the question "Should I Go Left?", those voting "Yes", their total count in percent may be 70% of the voters, and is called the "sample mean" of the result or the vote, and this sample mean equals YES (all letters capitalized) as the symbol used for the result of the vote result mean, whose traditional symbol is u. This simplification in names makes it easy for the casual reader to understand the mathematics. In Binomial probability, YES is associated with success, and NO is associated with failure. So if YES is p, and NO is q, then the traditional equation written as p + q = 1, becomes YES + NO = 1, and NO = 1 - YES. Example: A vote is taken by the congress, and 70% of the members vote "yes" and 30% vote "no", we have YES = 70% and NO = 30%, and YES + NO = 100%. I commence from this distraction.

How much risk will you accept from a stranger telling you what to do? How much confidence do you want in others' advice? Is the near-zero-confidence of a 50% to 50% vote or 51% to 49% vote or 60% to 40% vote an acceptable level? Take few minutes to understand the graphs.

A 50% to 50% vote result has nearly the same guidance confidence level as a 51% to 49% vote result, which is zero. And has zero information value.

Objects with zero value belong to the trash can.

This graph alone when understood should increase your understanding dramatically. Your political, law, social, and analytical ability will also increase. It is like looking at the road or earth ahead of you, and seeing flatness, and someone gives you the whole picture of earth from space and you realize the earth is not flat, it is a sphere. It is a revolution in realization and turns thinking in a completely different direction. And looking at the picture more closely, you realize, yes, a sphere, but more accurately it is an ellipse. Wow. What have I been educated and thinking all these years? The earth is not flat as many in history believed before. How could my education have been so wrong? How much error they caused in my life, and our lives, by such education? A vote that has 50% or 51% has near zero confidence and near 100% risk. A law adopted or a person elected by 51% YES support has near 0% confidence in its correctness, and therefore, has near 100% risk. This is a severely flawed voting system, and is the "Simple Majority" voting system used almost worldwide, or slight variations of it. The world is using a severely flawed system for its public decisions, whether to make laws, elect officials or in other domains.

Let us look at why this is so important. The following examples on deciding, selecting, or voting will be our start. They may sound repetitive, but this serves a purpose:

A surgeon succeeds in his operations 6 times out of 11 operations. He fails 5 operations out of 11. Do you ask a doctor his success rate before choosing? Is his success rate related to his quality (accuracy)? And is this an amount of risk we can accept?

A lawyer succeeds in his court cases 6 trials out of 11. He fails 5 trials out of 11. Do you ask a lawyer his success rate before choosing? Is his success rate related to his quality (accuracy)?

A civil engineer succeeds 6 times out of 11 times raising buildings or bridges he designs. He fails 5 buildings or bridges out of 11. Do you ask him his success rate before choosing? Is his success rate related to his quality? Is this an acceptable success rate? Is this a good accuracy level?

 The high school you choose for you son or daughter. 6 students out of 11 graduate and continue to study at universities. 5 students out of the 11 never finish high school or beyond. Do you ask this high school principal about their success rate before choosing? Is their success rate related to their quality? Is this a good accuracy level?

The university you choose for you son or daughter. 6 students out of 11 finish and graduate. 5 students out of the 11 never finish graduating. Do you ask them about their success rate before choosing?

The university you choose for you son or daughter. 6 students out of 11 after graduation are offered jobs immediately. 5 students out of the 11 are not offered jobs and struggle to find one. Do you ask the university about their job-finding success rate of the graduates after graduation? Another University nearby you did not choose for you son or daughter. 11 students out of 11 finish and graduate. 11 out of the 11 are offered jobs immediately upon graduation. Do you ask the university about such success rate before selecting a university for your child?

Music equipment produce pure (distortion-free) sound in 6 out of 11 brands. The bad sound part, called "Distortion", is at high level, in 5 out of 11 brands. Do you ask or look in the manual about the "Distortion Level" before choosing? Etc. for your car quality, refrigerator.

If you have not asked about the success and failure rates, how are you able to obtain an exact number to know the quality (accuracy of these tools)? Such poor selection ability by you can cost you greatly. The things you or your children or loved ones use could have possibly been of much higher quality if you knew what to ask or look for in a product. Could your father have altered your life if he sent you to another school? Are you choosing the best school for your children, and the best doctor for your parents, and the best lawyer for legal problems, etc.? Do you understand that a single inferior selection by you for a school for your child or you can effect whether that person is more likely to drop out before finishing high school, or go on to finish university, or finish university and excel in life? So by choosing the proper school, seemingly a very simple choice issue, you are deciding in great part the success or failure of your child in life.

Do you know that not choosing the better eye or heart doctor for your parent may produce blindness or death instead of good vision and a healthy heart for a healthy life? Do you know the joy value of a good music sound system with speakers that produce near-distortion-free music and sound versus poor quality music equipment? What is the accumulated cost of your poor selection over a lifetime? It can be extremely high, and makes the difference between having a successful satisfying life versus being a failure or having a life far below your potential. If you do not care about yourself, or too late for you, do you not care about your children or family being better equipped for success in life? Understanding some very simple basics about how to select can go a long way in this regard.

These direct costs of your choices should be clearly visible in your private life and are very personal to you. Similarly, the same poor quality laws and individuals you choose in public life, not only harm you, but they harm me also, because you do not know some basic things about voting and choosing, and about public elections, and the law. Take a moment to digest all this. Examples in choosing:

Choosing a surgeon:

Doctor, may I ask how many operations you have performed similar to the health problem I face?

Doctor answers: "many"

Doctor, would you be kind to give me a specific exact number? Do you not keep track of the number of operations you perform?

Doctor answers: "100 operations"

Doctor, may I ask how many of these operations were a success?

Doctor answers: "80" operation, 80% success rate.

Doctor, can you tell me about the 20% failure rate, what was the problem for that?

The doctor can then explain the reasons, which should be valuable information to you about the factors involved in the operation.

You can decide immediately or say "Thank you doctor for providing this information, I want to think about all this, and I may want to have a second or third opinion, and will make a final decision."

The same questions above can be asked of a lawyer, an engineer, a car or stereo salesman, the school principal of a potential school for you or your child. To assess quality, you need to know:

1. The amount of operations, or trials, or units involved

2. The success rate

3. The failure rate

4. Why the failure rate.

Now let us understand the importance of this information:

Statement 1: These four factors above when obtained should help you make the best decision

Statement 2: Best decisions should lead to best results

Statement 3: Your life path is in great part the result of a series of small and big decisions your parents have made, or you have made

Conclusion: By learning and applying these simple principles, you improve the quality of your life dramatically, and if you have children, you effect their life path even more dramatically, because it is not too late for them.

Doctors, Lawyers, Engineers, Mechanics, professionals would help the customer if they provide these four or first three facts readily, even maybe posted on their door. Some may have incentives not to do so, but the successful professionals should not shy from providing this data. The other task is to

1. Make sure the data is legitimate and not contrived and

2. Have a definition for what success means: For a surgeon, or a customer, success can be 100 percent end of the problem or 90 percent improvement, etc. For a school, success can mean the student graduates, or success can mean the student graduates and finds a job easily after graduation, which is a sign that the school is respected in the job market.

I now continue with the subject of voting. Both the YES group and NO group in a vote provide information that can be valuable. Almost universally in all countries, in voting on proposed laws or electing officials, the NO part of the vote is completely ignored, and the focus is on the YES group if they have enough support to cross the needed threshold to win, which may be 51% or 60% etc.

Let us look at why the NO group part of the vote is important, and should be an integral part in the vote equation. Suppose you asked for direction at that same fork of the road. At 51% YES, they win, if it was a vote in the USA congress (The House) or maybe a parliament. The NO group loses, and the proposed law is approved. But if we want to use the full information represented in the vote, we need to ask the NO voters some question: Why are you voting NO, and how serious the consequences are if the YES group wins? The NO group answers, saying: We have been living in this town much longer then those YES voters, and many times when it rains, about one mile on the left road, it creates a mud slide, and it causes a cliff in the road about 20 meters deep. The cliff is just after a road turn, and is difficult to see day time, and worse at night. This does not happen every times it rains, but often.

Now the vote has passed and the YES group won. If accepting their win is mandatory and now you have to select the left road while driving, you very likely will have a very bad accident, that may even be deadly. If the vote was about providing free biscuits to school children, and passed by 51% YES, the YES vote may be incorrect, but will you look at the two votes the same? The first vote will likely put you in an immediate horrible car accident and regarding the second vote will cost you little money where you have plenty of time to try to revoke the biscuits vote, without immediate great physical danger. I would like you to start thinking with wider view about voting, because the current way of evaluating voting results is highly flawed as I will explain. While the graphs show the risk range of a vote result, we will focus on votes from the results 50% YES to 50% NO and up, meaning, 60% YES, 70% YES, and up, because that is how winning is defined.

Same as being given water to drink. We should know how good the water quality is, such as 95% good, and 5% not good. The 5% not good part of the water is equivalent to the NO part of a vote. This 5% of the water can be polluted with sand, or salt, which effects only the taste and we can drink the water, which is unpleasant but low risk, but if the 5% pollution was toxic, such as maybe poison contaminated, then, we may absolutely refuse to accept the water, as high risk and deadly, even though this 5% is so much smaller than the good part of the water which is 95%. Therefore, it is important to know first the amount pollution in the water, and second the toxicity level of this pollution. Two factors are involved here, and need to be measured in the water and the food and similarly in the votes we consume: Pollution level, and this pollution's toxicity level. Toxicity is a danger level or risk level. So in the above vote example, the NO part of the vote can be seen as the vote pollution level, such as "your car may have problems if you choose the left road", which may be a minor concern because cars have problems often, but the warning from the NO group in the vote continues, saying " The problems will be from your car falling off a cliff while driving". This is the danger level or degree in a vote or advice or decision, similar to a toxicity level or danger level in water or food. We need to understand that both sides of the information in the vote may be important, and we need to learn how to compute these factors mathematically, so that we can make good, precise, scientifically calculated judgement.

Here I may have used the terms, "Information value", "Confidence", "Quality", "Certainty", "Risk", "Pollution level", "Toxicity", "Danger", "Accuracy" to describe some qualities of a vote. "Risk" means "risk coming from error level or danger level, or from pollution level and toxicity level" and "confidence" means confidence level.

The confidence level in a vote can be a measure of its quality. If the calculated confidence level in a vote is high, the quality of the vote should be high. If the calculated confidence is low, the quality of the vote should be considered low. So the words Confidence and Quality are strongly related. The higher the quality of the water or food, the more confident we are to use it, but the quality of the water or food must be measured scientifically, and then our confidence is well placed. So if we can measure with accuracy the quality of the water and food, we can decide more confidently whether to use it or not. To help remember this new way of looking at voting, we will simply say: **The quality of the water, food, decisions, and votes we use should be of good quality**. This seems like a common sense statement to help us remember the importance of the mathematics that measures the quality of a vote.

The quality of a vote is a measure of our calculated confidence in it. This confidence should be mathematically defined, and not be a general intuition. It is a computed measure that should be attached to every vote result. Without this measure attached, we cannot assess the usability of a vote. It is like water bottle given to you to drink. First, we need to know if the water is contaminated or clean, and need an accurate measure to describe the quality of the water. If this information is missing, we cannot make a good and confident decision on drinking it, because the water may be polluted or deadly to drink. When looking at a vote result, it is more important to look at its quality first, to know if it is usable or not. Therefore, attaching a vote quality, a vote accuracy number to every vote result, is like putting a quality number on a water bottle. This should be rule number one for your congress or parliament, your company board of directors, or your supreme court, or other courts votes. Does it make sense? If yes, why has it not been implemented yet? Because no formulas to compute this exist? OK. Let us create the formulas:

Which Way To The Hospital Emergency Room, Left Or Right?

Quality Of The Vote Result:

50%-50%= 0%   They Dont Know. Confidence is 0%. Risk is 100%. Useless advice.

51%-49%= 2%   They Dont Know. Practically the same as a 50%-50% vote. Useless.

60%-40%= 20% Uncertain Advice. Cannot trust.

80%-20%= 60% Confidence is improving.

95%-5% = 90% Confidence is better. Maybe they know.

99%-1% = 98% OK. Maybe I can trust your advice now.

100%-0% = 100% Best they can do. Confidence is 100%. Risk is 0%. I will follow it. I hope they are correct.

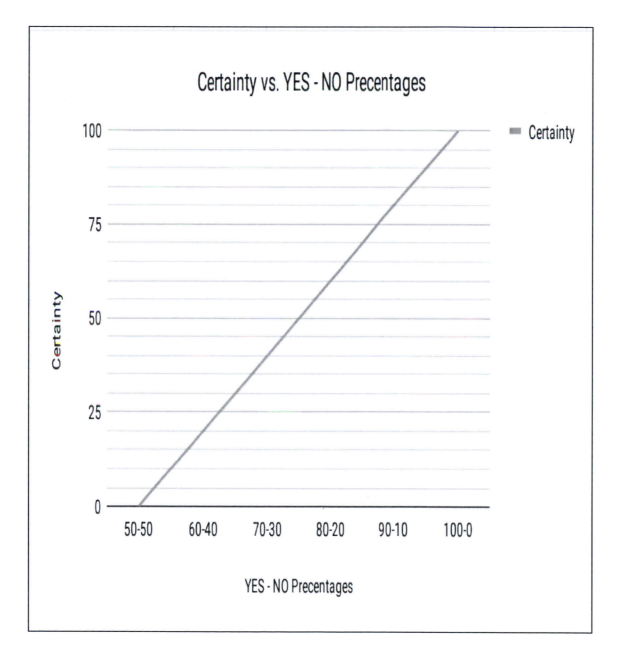

Note that Confidence or Certainty is the complement (somewhat like **opposite)** of Risk. If one is low the other is high. If confidence level is low, risk level is high. If confidence level is high, risk level is low. **Risk I define as:**

Risk = 100% minus Confidence

Example:

For a **50% YES to 50% NO vote:**

Confidence = 0%, because 50% chance Left minus 50% chance right = 0% confidence whether to choose Left or Right. Also at that point, the **Risk = 100%**, (from the formula 100% minus 0% = 100%). It is logical the risk of going Left or Right is maximum at 100%, because the chance of error is maximum.

Scientists may use technical terms such as "Randomness" or "Entropy", while in Statistics the word Confidence Level is used, and they would say that "at 50% to 50% equal chance of correct result for choosing Left or Right, the randomness is maximum and the Confidence Level is minimum at 0%. Technical words that also mean: The results are useless for deciding intelligently, or, the results are like a random result, or a flip of a coin to make a decision, and we should not do this unless we are gambling about correctness of a decision. If the decision comes up correct, it is pure "luck" and not "intelligence". So "luck" is equivalent to a random decision that turns out to be correct, while what we want in life are decisions based on intelligence and not luck. An airplane and most useful tools are designed and function based on intelligence, not luck. But let me keep the language simple and continue. Example 2:

For a **51% YES to 49% NO vote** by heart doctors if the patient needs an operation. Those opposing doctors say NO, not needed, simple pills in few months solve the problem:

Confidence = 2%, because 51% minus 49% = 2%

Risk = 98%, because 100% minus 2% = 98%

The operation costs $100,000, is full of risk of death from operation complications, while the pills cost $1000 and are said to be safe and produce good results. Now, will you follow the 51% calling for the operation just because they are a numerical majority? Or will you say, 51% to 49% advice is practically the same as 50% to 50% decision? Both groups of voters do not give much **confidence** or **certainty**, so you try to play it safe, and probably choose the pills. But if the decision was 95% to 5%, then you may feel more confident or certain about how to proceed, operate or not, go Left or go Right, etc.

Instead of the choices being go left or go right, if it were a vote in parliament or congress on a subject, and the two choices were YES in favour of a proposed law, or vote NO if you oppose, then the same logic applies. An abstention vote is counted as a No vote, because the voter does not know the good choice. To minimize risk, an abstention is counted as a NO vote. As a practical matter, absent votes can be counted as a NO, or have no count, and this effects the voters group size and related issues. An example is law makers deciding on a proposed law to ban cigarettes. 50 percent of law makers vote YES and 50 percent vote NO. In mathematics, the formula is simple: Numbers voting YES minus numbers voting NO equals the amount of difference between the two groups voting. The vote result is zero in this case. It is typical to describe the result of such a vote in congress as a 50% to 50% vote, but this is extremely misleading because the total tally of the vote is zero.

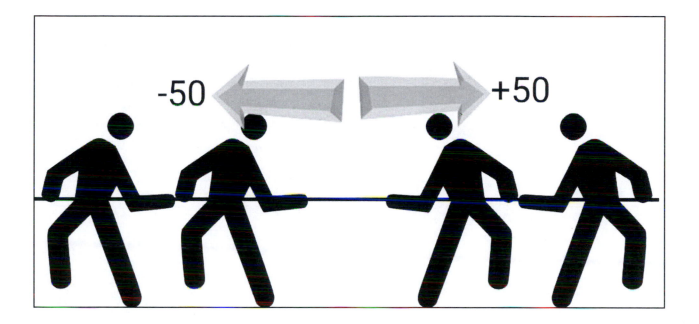

A vote by a person has "a value and has a direction". The value of a YES vote is +1, which is a value of 1 pointing in the positive direction. The value of a NO vote is -1, which is a value of 1 pointing in the opposite direction, which is 180 degrees opposed. It is like a rope game with two groups opposing each other pulling on the rope to see who will win (Tug Of War game). One person's power on one side equals 1 in value, and the other person pulling in the opposite direction has power that equals -1. So at 50 persons on one side and 50 persons on the other side, the result in power is zero. It is not good to describe the total result as 50-to-50. When adding a vote total, it is important to add an opposing vote as a negative number, and the total count of the vote becomes zero. The opposing powers of 50 plus -50 totals 0 in value. They cancel each other and no one wins. So the vote (or advice) in this case provides no useful information on how to proceed, go left or go right, showing that these people collectively have no good answer that we may use.

What is extremely important and central to understand here is: It is the difference in numbers between the two groups that matters. This difference must be represented in percentage.

A more proper graphical representation of the equation is this:

The illustration above is not a Tug Of War, where when one group overpowers another group they win, for example 60 people on one side overpowers 40 people on the other side, assuming every person has equal power, as in voting, where a person's power equals one vote. Therefore, in a Tug Of War, 60 people overpower 40 people and the game is over and they win. But in a poll, 60 people out of 100 represent 60% and 40 people out of 100 represents 40%, and when the 60% win, the net power of the poll is = 60% - 40% = 20%. Why is this the important number? Think of a carriage or a car being pulled by horses or human. 60 people or horses pulling the car in one direction and 40 people pulling the car in the opposite direction. The net power the car has is 20 horsepower or 20 humanpower. The vote by these 100 people as input, produced only 20 as useful output. If the results were 70 to 30, then the vote accuracy would be 70% - 30% = 40%. 40% is much higher accuracy than 20% accuracy, but still seems very low. What we would like is high accuracy of maybe 90%, 95% or 99% etc., or best is 100%. This means, that to reach these levels, such as 96% accuracy, the vote results must be 98% to 2%, which is 98% - 2% = 96% accuracy. Note how high the vote results for "In Favour" have to be in order to achieve an accuracy level that is so much higher than 20%. Now, a 60% to 40% vote looks unacceptable as a standard. Would you want your computer or airplane or gun to have 20% accuracy? Would even a 96% accuracy be enough? What if the issue is a death sentence? Are you willing to accept your father be sentenced by a computer that has 96% accuracy? Therefore, what we like in general is high accuracy in important matters, and high accuracy means smart design. A "poll" or a "vote'" is a tool, and we need to have this tool have high accuracy, or equivalently in this illustration, high efficiency, or no waste of energy. A car engine with 20% efficiency is not a good car engine. For a vote, this tells us the vote results are not good, and cannot be known accurately, or with confidence, and the vote should be rejected. We would like

100% confidence if possible or 99% confidence, and then we may feel satisfied with the decision that comes out of the poll.

More examples: We give a gambler $100 to gamble with in order to test his gambling skills or intelligence in deciding. On a successful bet he wins $1. On a failed bet he loses $1. He succeeds 60 bets out of 100 bets or 60% of the bets. The number of the bets is not what we care about as a result. We care about how much money he wins and brings home. Therefore, the "input" is $100 that we gave him, and the "output" we look for is money won. How much did this person win in money? Did he win $60? No! He succeeded in 60 bets and failed in 40 bets. He won $60 minus the lost $40, for a net of $20. This person won only $20 to take home! We can compute his win as percent Success - percent Failure = 60% - 40% = 20%.

Same for a senator gambling that he has good idea, and wants the senators to adopt it. We give him 100 senators' vote to play with. He presents his idea, and he wins 60 votes, or 60%. But we must not forget how much he lost. He lost 40 votes or 40%. Therefore his win is percent Success - percent Failure = 60% - 40% = 20%! This simple formula gives voting a very different result than what is traditionally announced as poll result, which is: The senator won 60% of the voters! This is a WRONG Poll Total Result, because he also lost 40%. His win is 20% of the voters. So if this person is smart or have correct ideas, why did he win only 20%? Why not win 40% or 60% or 80% or 100% of the voters. Is it low intelligence? He is either not smart, or has incorrect ideas, or is not able to communicate his ideas well. In any case, he failed and the result shows it. He won 20%, and he is as good as an engine with 20% efficiency, which should be considered a very bad engine.

I have given many analogies because this issue is extremely important to understand. When we understand this fully, then we begin to understand why it should be unacceptable to elect an official or a law by low Poll Results, such as 20% or 50% or 70%, etc. For an engine, it is a bad design. For a gambler, he is not a smart chooser. For a person seeking office, he is not an intelligent person, and for a proposed law, it is a bad idea.

No matter how we look at this kind of vote, where both opposing sides are equal in number, the results we get are zero:

- Zero for the "total count" of the vote

- Zero for the "physics power" of the vote

- Zero for the "information value" of the vote

- Zero for the "amount of difference" between the two opposing groups numbers

- Zero for the "confidence value" the vote provides

"Guidance" may be a good term to use because in life, we seem to be looking for guidance sometimes or giving guidance to our loved ones on how to proceed, go left or go right so-to-speak on many decisions. If your child asked the family for direction on an issue, and 5 out of 10 members said "do this" and the other 5 family members said "do the opposite", that is not good guidance the child can use. A proper reaction by the child is to be confused and to say to himself, my family does not know this issue well, because if they did, they would all be telling me the same. The child can ask "Should I finish high school or university or take this job offer?" If 5 said "finish school" and the other 5 said the opposite "do not finish school, take the job", then the child may wisely say, the "guidance" of the poll I have taken has little value to me, because my family members are either confused, and they should tell me "we do not have a good answer or know a good answer". Both sides think they are correct and care about their child, but the poll mathematics, shows the results of the poll as not usable to guide us in the decision. When all 10 family members say "finish school" or "do not finish school", the child can be more confident in the guidance and more comfortable in making a decision based on this poll result. I have given you several analogies to help you understand this new and important concept. Therefore, the accuracy of a poll is related to the value of its guidance. And a poll of 50% to 50% gives no guidance, while a poll of 100% to 0% gives maximum (best) guidance. Notice that it does not matter if the 100% is "finish school" or "do not finish school". The accuracy does not tell you if the decision is correct. Either side may be correct. The accuracy tells you "we may be correct or not, but this is the best information we can give you." If the child and family have no money or options, the child may choose "not finish school", if all 10 members tell him this, and since this is usually a terrible choice, the person may finish school at a later time or do self-study, or he may choose to "finish school" if all 10 members vote "finish school". In either choice, there is more confidence in the guidance that is the result of this family poll. The poll makes no judgment, it is a tool, and can be used to provide a probability about the accuracy of the poll results.

From these facts, we can see that a 50% to 50% vote is the worst possible vote result a congress, parliament, jury, court, Supreme Court, or a committee can have, because it gives no good guidance on the issue voted on. It is the lowest absolute total count value possible with the lowest absolute vote confidence value. Therefore, such a vote is a zero on the scale of vote value and should be dismissed as not usable. But how is a 50% to 50% vote result different from a 51% to 49% vote result? Are they practically the same and useless? A huge light bulb should start to light up in your mind if you figured it out. But let us continue.

- From this lowest value point on the scale of vote evaluation, we start to move upward very slowly in the value and usability of a vote as we will see.

-

40

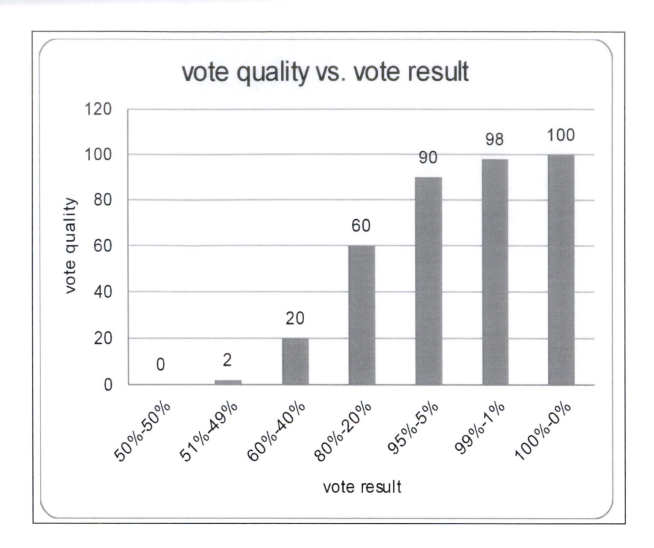

Vote Total = percent of Yes voters - percent of No votes = %Yes - %No

Example: 10 voters vote on an issue. 6 of them vote Yes, and 4 vote No. Breaking this down, we get

Vote Total = 1 + 1 + 1 + 1 + 1 + 1 - (1 + 1 + 1 + 1) = 6 - 4 = 2 out of 10 voters = 20%

Targets and Errors. Mathematics you can ignore.

A target for a political candidate is 100% support in a poll. For a Supreme Court judge or group of them, the target is 100% support for the argument when a poll among the court judges is held in a trial, etc. On the other side of human guessing, the opposing humans to a candidate or an issue, the target is 0%, that is, their target is the failure of the candidate or issue. While it is typical to think of a target as just winning, the Ideal Target is the proper target mathematically, when we try to maximize accuracy in the vote's result. Although 51% support may get you a win, but the confidence of the voters in your win may 0%, and many voters may look down on such a win, as a lucky win, and not a mathematically credible or legitimate win. When a candidate or law or decision is adopted, the maximum accuracy in the vote should be the target or goal, and this means the target of the vote should be 100%. With the introduction of a target, the idea of error becomes concrete and measurable. **Error becomes the distance away in percent of a result (or measure) from the target**. If a candidate gets 60% support in a poll, then the error is 100% - 60% = 40%. However, in polls, there are two parts, and both parts need to be entered in the error equation. One part is those persons supporting the issue, and their target is 100% success and the other part are those opposing the issue and their target is the 0% side of the interval, that is, they want 100% opposition to the issue, so it would fail. So the errors are the distance of those supporting the issue from 100% target, plus the error of those opposing the issue from the 0% target.

The Yes voters have a target of 100% support for the vote, which are 10 votes. But they missed their target by 4 votes and achieved only 6 votes which are 60%. So the error for them is = 10 - 6 = 4 out of 10, or 40% error.

The No voters have a target of 0% support for the vote, because they oppose it. But they missed their target by 4 votes and achieved only 4 votes or 40%. The error for them is 4 - 0 = 4 or 40% error.

Notice that the two errors of the Yes group and No group are equal. The total error is therefore The Yes group error + The No group error

= %No + %No

= 2 x %No

= 2 x 40%

= 80% error in the vote

Since Accuracy = 100% - Error

Vote Accuracy = 20%

This is the same as the Vote Total we calculated first above.

Therefore: Vote Accuracy = Vote Total

This is a very simple, remarkable, and very significant result.

The Accuracy Of The Vote = The Vote Total in percentages

As a formula, we write it as

Vote Accuracy = %Yes voters - %No voters

= Vote Total in percent

Vote Accuracy = Vote Total in percent

Therefore, when you total your vote accurately, using the method provided here, you are getting the vote accuracy as well.

Now you have taken the first simple, but gigantic step towards making voting a science.

A side note: In statistics the term "Confidence Level" is used, and it is NOT the same as accuracy, but there is a relationship between the two terms. Accuracy of the vote is the proper measure, but some times, I am using the terms interchangeably, because common people can relate to this term more than to the accuracy term. The complete accuracy formula is much more comprehensive and relevant than the Confidence Level formula. Yet another technical issue that you can ignore for now, until you read my technical text book, if you want to know the exact difference.

You can ignore this, but here is the mathematical proof for the curious:

Vote Ideal Accuracy = 100% - (%No + %No) = 100% - %No - %No

Since %Yes + %No = 100%

%No = 100% - %YES,

Substituting for %NO, we get

Accuracy = 100% - %No - (100% - %Yes) = %Yes - %No

Total Vote Accuracy = %Yes - %No

(Reference : Jamil Kazoun, the book "A Mathematical Foundation For Politics And Law")

In our example: The Vote Accuracy is simply the 60% Yes voters - 40% No voters = 20% !

The Vote Accuracy = 20%

So simple and so powerful a mathematical result.

So we know a vote with 50% Yes to 50% No has 0% Accuracy

But what does a vote with 51% Yes to 49% No has in accuracy?

Vote Accuracy = 51% - 49% = 2% accuracy

Wow! 2% accuracy is so close to 0% accuracy, that we may as well call it that, 0% accuracy. It is useless.

And you may suddenly realize that 51% Yes to 49% No, sounds a lot like what is called "The Simple Majority Voting System", and you may also suddenly remember that most people in the world tend to use The Simple Majority Voting System. Then, a sharp pain may hit your head, as you realize, that most of the world is using a decision system, a voting system, that guarantees nothing more than 0% in accuracy.

Now it is ok to stop, yell, scream, and say "Is this real?"

Time to take a break, a long break, for a drink, a cup of coffee or something.

We continue. But what about a vote with 70% Yes to 30% No?

Vote Accuracy = 70% -30% = 40% accuracy.

How would you like your car breaking system to be 40% of the time accurate? This means 60% of the time it is inaccurate. Or your parachute opening mechanism system to be 40% of the time accurate? Or your airplane control system to be 40% of the time accurate? Or your watch to be 40% of the time accurate? Or your computer to be 40% of the time accurate?

All of a sudden, a vote with 70% Yes support, that normally is celebrated as a major success, seems like a total disaster! This vote seems to have an unacceptable amount of error and should be a total reject for any important tool or decision.

With this simple formula, the world of politics as practiced today, has just been turned upside down on its head, and maybe even mortally destroyed.

I should say a quick word here about the term "Accuracy" of a vote. When 50 people are telling you to go one way and the other fifty telling you to go the opposite way, how confident can you be about the correctness of their combined advice? The answer is zero confident, because you do not have a basis on which to decide which group to choose. And making a choice when there is not much confidence in the provided choices is making an error. That is what the terms "Accuracy" relates to. Certainty or confidence or accuracy in general are words used to represent the opposite of randomness, as an antonym. Randomness is when you toss a coin, to decide which way to proceed on the road, and it gives zero confidence about the choice, because it is based on a "random guess" of a 50-to-50 chance that has no intelligence in it. For a vote of 50% support to 50% oppose, the randomness is maximum, that is, the lack of knowledge is maximum. The error in your decision, if you chose at this point, is maximum, and your accuracy is minimum. So flipping a coin with 50% chance of getting HEADS is a similar result to such a vote result and is a bad way to make decisions on important matters, and that is the situation being practiced in congresses and parliaments as I will elaborate.

The word "difference" also means "different". In life and learning or making decisions, the question we often ask is what is the difference between this object and that? The Difference Measure is the opposite of the Similarity Measure. So we can ask what is the difference between yellow and green? Between circle and triangle, between a high school graduate and a college graduate. Example: If you want to see a doctor. And two doctors are available and went to the same university and graduated at age 25 and received equal grades. But one doctor's age is 25 and the other doctor's age is 35. How do you choose between them? You may ask what is the difference between the first doctor and the second. One difference is experience. The first doctor's age is 25 and he graduated at age 25, so he has zero years experience. The second doctor is 35 and graduated at age 25 so he has 10 years experience. So the question of what is different between the first doctor and the second is 10 years experience. Is this an important number? It is important because all other factors being equal, this doctor is probably better. If the first doctor was 27 years old, that means he had 2 years experience as a doctor. This may be better than zero experience but compared to 10 years experience, I may still prefer the second doctor. If the first doctor had 9 years experience, then it may not make much of a difference because they have nearly the same amount of experience. When choosing which of these two doctors is better, it is not the amount of experience each doctor has that matters in making a decision, but the "**amount of difference**" in experience between the two doctors. If the **amount of difference** is big, we choose the one with more experience, but if the

48

amount of difference is zero or small, we may not know which doctor to choose, because relative to each other, they are nearly the same, and we will not know which is better. Both may be good or both may be bad, etc. But when the difference between them is large, we are more comfortable with the decision, because one doctor seems relatively much better than the other doctor. Let us create a simple table of this situation:

The first doctor has 0 years experience minus 10 years experience by the second doctor equals 10 years difference.

The first doctor has 2 years experience minus 10 years experience by the second doctor equals 8 years difference.

The first doctor has 9 years experience minus 10 years experience by the second doctor equals 1 year difference.

We can understand in this case what is different between two numbers, or said differently the distance between them, by using the Difference Measure operator which for numbers is subtraction. **Then we look at this difference to decide. We ask if this difference is big, medium, small and how it effects the issues involved**. But having explained all this about the two doctors, it is important to know that our accuracy formula does not apply when comparing two doctors. Our formula only works for evaluating one doctor at a time. So the question we could ask voters is "is this doctor good, Yes or No?". From their answer, we can compute accuracy. Notice that the critical factor in the question is relating to one issue, not two, and the choices are {Yes , No}. This is almost always the case in law making, where is question usually is "do you support adopting this proposal as a law, Yes or No?", and in a court the vote is similarly limited to {Yes , No}, where the question typically is " do you find the accused guilty, Yes or No?". But in elections, when more than one candidate is involved, the accuracy formula does not work, as I explain at the end of the book, because of "vote splitting". If an election had two candidates, and both are extremely acceptable to the voters, but one of the candidates wears a white tie and the other a blue tie, and 50% of voters like white ties and vote for one candidate and the other 50% of voters like blue ties, and vote for the other candidate, then each candidate will get 50% of the votes and neither can win, or if they win, their win has low accuracy. The vote was decided based on a trivial factor: The color of the candidates' tie, when other factors are far more important. But if the vote was regarding a single candidate " Do you approve of this candidate, Yes or No?", Then the candidate may get 99% support for a very credible win. Therefore, when voting, even if the previous voting round was a comparison vote, there needs to be a final round in which the vote is " on a single subject with {Yes or No} as the options. Therefore, in elections, if more than two candidates are involved, there should be a final round where the chosen candidate is voted on alone in a final round. We diverged slightly from our focus, but this helps to add clarity as to when we can use the accuracy formula.

Going back to our law-makers' voting example, and I will use the word vote and advice interchangeably, I ask: How do we choose which voting group has the better advice about road directions? The group voting YES (go left) or the group voting NO (do not go left)? I ask: What is different between a 50 percent YES and 50 percent NO vote? The answer is: **no difference or zero difference in numbers. Their advice is useless as to how to proceed, left or right**.

As soon as we move away from this lowest point on the voting scale, look what happens. If forty-nine percent had said you should take the right road, and fifty-one percent of them said you should take the left road, would you feel comfortable following the fifty-one percent group, even if it is a win for them? How much confidence would you have that fifty-one percent of the congressmen were correct? Not much! After all, the difference between the two groups equals 2 percent. **2 percent difference is an extremely small amount of difference and for all practical reasons can be considered to be the same as zero percent difference**. If it happened that two percent of the congressmen had voted the other way, the fifty-one percent vote would have gone in the other direction and so would the advice. In other words, even if fifty-one percent are telling you to take the left road, the fifty-one percent are nearly equally likely to be wrong, as they are to be right. It is almost as if we are still in the 50-to-50 percent toss of the coin situation. We need a much bigger difference before we can start to think: maybe this groups really knows better than the opposing group. So immediately, the question of the size of the difference, the amount of difference, becomes the issue that gives us comfort in the advice's accuracy. So a difference of 2 % is not important, but a difference of 30%, or 60% or 100% is increasingly better, and gives more and more **confidence** to you that these people know what they are talking about. So to summarize: **We should desire or require to see a big amount of difference between the voting groups, when a vote is taken. The bigger this difference is, the higher is the level of confidence that the advice is useable**. For example, if the vote was eighty percent "IN FAVOUR" of going left, and twenty percent "OPPOSED", you may start to feel more comfortable about taking the left road, and following the eighty percent, because looking at the amount of difference, of eighty percent in favour minus twenty percent opposed, we get a sixty-percent difference between the two views which is much better than zero amount of difference we had been talking about before. So the situation is improving for this man seeking advice, but is this enough improvement?

Let us stay with this example for a while. What if eighty percent of these congressmen said go left, and twenty percent opposed, but your final destination was only a coffee shop that was two hundred meters away? You would probably not be too concerned about how correct they are and about making a mistake, because the stakes are a lot lower. If the voters were wrong, about two hundred meters down the road you can make a turn, come back and take the other road. A small amount of gasoline and time spent. So you don't think much about it. The cost of a mistake is low.

Now, let us assume instead that your destination is about two hundred kilometers away on a one-way road. Are you going to be quick to take the advice of the eighty percent of the congressmen telling you to take the left road? You may start to think: "What if the eighty percent are wrong?" Knowing the cost of making the wrong choice is higher, you are going to be very hesitant about taking their advice.

Now, let us assume that your destination is two hundred kilometers away on a one-way road, and you are going to a hospital because you just got a phone call that your mother is in the emergency room and may die in few hours if you cannot get to her. Now, which advice would you take on choosing the road? Imagine making such an important decision in life on a vote of eighty percent versus twenty percent. The amount of difference in this vote, the amount of sixty percent difference is no longer comforting. It no longer gives you enough confidence about how to proceed. Now you require more confidence from the vote. Now, you want these congressmen to tell you which way to proceed with 95% confidence level. Or much more comforting, **because it is a life and death decision regarding your mother, you would like the vote to be 99% or best 100% certain. This is one of the most important facts you may need to remember in your life about decision making and about the law, law-making and voting**. How in the world can you accept and have been accepting systems of governments that make decisions based on near zero confidence level of accuracy or two percent confidence level of accuracy, and are happy with that, when what you really want or should demand from people when making important decisions is for them to provide a high level of confidence of being correct in their advice, in their votes? How has this happened to you, to your neighbours , to your town and city fellow citizens, or your fellow countrymen, to you city hall representatives, and congresses and parliaments? Stop for a moment to absorb all this, if you can!!!!!!!!

I hope that you are starting to see the point. When you make a decision, it is most important that the decision have a high level of confidence of being accurate. And one way we measure this confidence level is not looking at the percentages of each group voting, but by looking at the amount of difference between the two voting groups. What is important is the percentage difference between those who are telling you to do one thing and those who are telling you to do the opposite, and we want this difference to be high enough, and ideally near 100% level. This difference is the confidence factor I define, and it is what we should look at or demand before we even know the subject matter of the vote is. We want the total vote count to be technical credible, as a first step in any vote. It is like going to a heart doctor for advice, and the very first thing you may want to know from the doctor is: Do you have a certificate of qualification from a medical institution that you are a qualified doctor or heart doctor? If not, you may immediately leave without further discussion to look for a qualified doctor. Similarly, when someone tells you there was a vote or advice vote on a subject, the first question to ask is: Did this vote have a high level of confidence numbers associated with it? If not, then the vote is not worth considering! Looking at your city hall, state hall, congress, or parliament, for an entire year's period, how many votes were passed with a respectable confidence level, such as 100%, 99% or even 95%? It is possible that not a single vote did! It is interesting to do such surveys just to see how many laws passed with near zero level of confidence, and to tabulate the vote confidence levels. A revolution in politics and law may follow if citizens understood the implications.

1st Factor

When making a decision or giving advice using a voting process and you do not know all the variables involved, there is chance of making an error. We should ask:

Is it a must that a vote be taken? Or can the vote be delayed until more information is available?

What is the minimum confidence level of the vote that must be achieved for the vote to be accepted? If not accepted, the vote is dismissed.

When a decision has to be made in that environment and it is to be a group decision by a vote, and the only options for the vote are YES or NO, or "In Favour" or "Opposed", then a reasonable formula I developed to measure the value of the vote is "The Merit Of The Vote", but a more usable public name to use is "The Quality Of The Vote" or a mathematical more suitable name is "The Accuracy Of The Vote".

The Accuracy Of The Vote I defined as the percentage of those voting "in favour" minus the percentage of those voting "opposed":

Accuracy = percent "In Favour" minus percent "Opposed"

At 50 percent YES against 50 percent NO vote, we get 50 minus 50 which equals 0, making the accuracy of this vote zero percent. This vote gives 0 guidance, level of confidence, (or information) on how to proceed. This zero percent accuracy is the lower bound on the accuracy scale. At 100 YES against 0 NO, we get 100 percent minus zero percent which gives 100 percent accuracy. This 100% accuracy is the upper bound of the accuracy scale. At 100% accuracy, the vote gives the maximum guidance (or information) possible on how to proceed. At 100% accuracy, we cannot do any better. The Accuracy Of The Vote says nothing about the subject content of the vote, and if the content is correct or not. The vote can be 100 YES against 0 NO, claiming the earth is flat, which is incorrect, but that is the best guidance (outcome) the voting system can produce. So we can have a vote with 100 percent accuracy, and still be 100 percent incorrect in content. Accuracy is related to the voter numbers, while law content accuracy is related to the subject of the law. The subject of the law voted on is something that voters may never be able to measure its correctness successfully. If we cannot know if the law's content is accurate, what do we do? There is not much we can do except take some comfort by looking at the accuracy of the vote. It is an important technical measure that is independent of content and is very useful to give guidance when looking at a vote, but is not a complete solution. Therefore, from this argument, we can conclude that laws are inherently uncertain in their content accuracy, and uncertain in their vote accuracy, and we can only compute a statistical level of confidence, but it is statistical and probabilistic in nature, and this is the flaw of the law. So I will create a definition of "The Flaw Of The Law" to be this:

We cannot measure the accuracy of a law with full confidence or accuracy, and if "justice" means accurate judgement, then The Law Is Inherently Flawed And Is Damaging If Used For Justice.

Some may argue that the law has benefits and costs, and we can try to balance these factors, but in this case, how do you calculate the cost to a particular citizen? **The amount of the cost may be zero to one citizen, while it can be enormous to another citizen**? How can you put this in your calculation? You will see that it is not possible because one person will sell his freedom for 1 dollar and another will die for his freedom. So **disposing with the law seems like a logical conclusion of these arguments.** Let individuals resolve their problems as best they can and are able to without government interference, and **let them make their own errors in settlement, not you forcing more error on them, unless you are a mediator chosen by both**.

We can ask: **How can a law court accept to use a law that has less than 100% merit or accuracy? And how can a jury of people or a jury of judges accept their own vote result if it has less than 100% merit? Is the court a place of justice or a gambling shop? It seems logical that either situation would be grounds to dismiss a case in court, or to dismiss the court.**

Please take few moments to understand what you have just encountered in these previous words. **The ramifications are enormous.** It is like for thousands of years, people believed the earth is flat and someone in few lines said "the earth is not flat, and here is why... "It is a complete opposite of common knowledge and common practice.

Here is the most basic (word) table for The Accuracy Of A Vote, for any vote and any subject, not accounting for the group size:

- **Fifty percent in favour, minus, fifty percent opposed, gives zero percent Accuracy**
- Sixty percent in favour, minus, forty percent opposed, gives twenty percent Accuracy
- Seventy percent in favour, minus, thirty percent opposed, gives forty percent Accuracy
- Eighty percent in favour, minus, twenty percent opposed, gives sixty percent Accuracy
- Ninety percent in favour, minus, ten percent opposed, gives eighty percent Accuracy
- One hundred percent in favour, minus, zero percent opposed, gives one hundred percent Accuracy

Do not you proceed any further in reading before you understand this table.

We can set threshold as to what is a low accuracy, a medium accuracy, an acceptable accuracy. For example:

If the accuracy of a vote is 0% to 95%, the vote has low accuracy, and the vote may be automatically rejected.

If the accuracy of the vote is 95% or higher, then the vote may be considered as having acceptable accuracy. There are other considerations such as the costs of making an error in the law, where the costs can be extremely high, and a higher confidence level may be demanded.

It is important to understand: Even when the accuracy of a vote is 100 percent, we still cannot be sure that the vote is a correct decision. Example: The congress may vote with 100% accuracy to assert that "the earth is flat" or to "require car drivers to wear helmets for additional safety", but the vote content can be incorrect. **What Accuracy Of The Law can mean in this bad case is: This is the best outcome the voting system can produce, and this outcome can be completely wrong sometimes**. You can have congress full of uneducated individuals producing many votes with 100% accuracy, but the content of these votes can still be 100% incorrect. In these cases, it would mean, the earth is not flat, and making helmets a requirement on car drivers is a bad idea, or an error. Sure wearing a helmet adds extra safety to the car driver? But are you considering the visible and hidden costs to him in your decision? Are you thinking of the cost of the helmet, how inconvenient it is for him to wear inside the car, especially in hot weather, if it effects his hearing ability to hear warning sounds from outside, the height of the ceiling in the car? Does the congress now require having cars with higher ceilings? Etc. And why not force the driver to wear additional protective clothing. All these add extra safety to the driver? And why not require all passengers to wear helmets and special protective clothing? These measures all increase safety. The short answer is that "how much risk I take in my life is my own damn business and it is not your business, or any other voter's business. If I want to sky dive, rock climb, parachute, white water raft, ride horses, ride motorcycles, skate board, swim in deep oceans, or what ever. You are not my father or mother and I am a mature adult, and mind your own damn business". But at this stage, we are not discussing philosophy, but mathematics and logic, and I will continue.

Therefore, a few important questions to ask are:

Should we mind our own business and not interfere in others business?

Do we have the right to interfere in such issues? Who or what gives us such rights?

Must a decision be made on the issue, knowing that decisions can be incorrect?

The formula for the Accuracy Of The Vote is extremely simple to compute and use. It may be very wise to keep it this way. But when the number of voters is small, a second error we have not talked about yet becomes important and needs to be added to the accuracy equation. In voting, the number of the voters is the group size and in statistics, it is called "'the sample size". In statistics, one of the most important discoveries is called "The Central Limit Theorem" which allows computing how many people are needed to have low error in a vote. In the recorded history of man, there is evidence that people instinctively knew that the more people participate in a decision, the higher the Confidence Level is in the decision. So maybe in a tribes, before a decision is made, the tribal chief creates a meeting with many tribe members to discuss a concern and asks for their guidance and vote on the issue, and the greater the number of people participating, the more everyone was comfortable with the final agreed upon decision. and in recent times, instead of having a single judge in court make the decision of guilt, which can have serious consequences, such as sentencing a person to death, and a judge being a single person, even if highly intelligent and educated can make mistakes, it became the norm in many places to have a jury composed of several people or several judges make the decision, instead of one person, with the idea that "the more persons are involved in a decision: 1. The higher the Confidence Level will be in the results, and 2. The lower the error in the decision will be." What statisticians or mathematicians were able to do as a result of this theorem, is to measure the exact error that a specific group size causes. So if a drug company tested a new medicine on only 3 people, The Confidence Level in the results would be very low and they could not make a 'credible' statement about the drug. But if the drug was tested on 100 people, their statement would have a higher Confidence Level. If the test was carried on 10000 people, then the Confidence Level will be much higher in the results. note that this Confidence Level says nothing about the drug! The company's statement when 10000 people are tested may be:

1. The drug was test and the result is "90% were cured, and we can say "We have very high Confidence Level the drug is effective"'.

2. The drug was test and the result is "10% were cured, and we can say "We have very high Confidence Level the drug is not effective"'.

3. The drug was test and the results were "50% were cured, and 50% became more sick, and we can say "We have very high Confidence Level that we do not know if the drug is effective or not effective"'.

Etc.

In all three statements, the company says "we have a high Confidence Level" regardless if the drug test results are good, bad, or undetermined. Having a high Confidence Level is related to the group size and is one required component of the accuracy equation. We already discussed the second required component, which is high percentage support or success. It is like making a cup of coffee, and it requires two components in sufficient amounts. It requires water, in sufficient amount. And it requires coffee (powder or beans etc.), in sufficient amount. Having water alone, or too little of it and you cannot have a cup of coffee, and having coffee alone, and too little of it, you cannot have a cup of coffee. Same for Percent Support in a vote and Confidence Level in a vote. Having Percent Support alone or too little of it, you cannot have accuracy, and having no Confidence Level or too little of it, and you cannot have accuracy. Confidence Level relates to the Group Size, and is a component of accuracy.

From this we can begin to understand the significance of having a large number of people participating in a vote. We can estimate the minimum number of people (group size) needed for a vote based on statistics formulas. So a congress or parliament may be required to have a minimum of 100 members in it.

The group size when we are evaluating a surgeon is the number of operations he has performed. If this number is 1, 3, 10, 100 or 1000, it gives us more confidence the bigger the number is. If he performs 1000 operations and they all fail, or they all succeed, it does not matter at this point! Either way, the data gives us more confidence in the computations to come, even though we do not yet know the conclusion. What if he only performed 3 operations? And we do not know their success outcome. If we knew the outcome, will we have much confidence that 3 operations are enough data to judge his accuracy? What if the next 3 operations he does all fail? Are 10 operations enough? How about 100 operations? These numbers, called in mathematics the "Sample Size", by themselves, are an important factor that gives a confidence level on whether they are large enough or not to use in our computations. And the bigger this sample number is, the more we can trust their conclusion. So when a surgeon says I had performed only three operations with 100% success rate, which in the Ideal Accuracy gives 100% accuracy, but we may still have little confidence about using the doctor for a critical heart or eye operation. But if this surgeon performed 1000 operations with 100% success rate, we will have high Ideal Accuracy AND low error produced from the sample size which in turn gives high Confidence Level about using him. Both Ideal Accuracy and Confidence Level are sufficiently high to make accuracy high.

A vote by a congress or a parliament or a court that is composed of 9 people will produce lots of error from the small group size even with 100% support in the vote. All their votes no matter the vote result will have high error and low accuracy because of the small group size. So for example, the U.S.A. Supreme Court has a group size of 9 voters as judges sitting on the bench. You will see shortly how to compute using a formula its group size error,and it is basically 32% error from having a jury of only 9 judges. This also assumes the vote is unanimous, as a criminal death sentence jury often requires because it a serious decision. We can assume that a Supreme Court decision is always extremely serious, because it often effects an entire country's population, not just one person. So if this court's minimal error is 32% this also means its maximum accuracy is 68%! This court no matter what it does cannot be more than 68% accurate. Add to this the errors that come from using the Simple Majority Voting instead of Unanimous Voting, and even other factors become important as you can see later at the end of the book. Just from this one factor, the group size, we can see that this court is a highly flawed institution, and this has nothing to do with ideology, and is a purely mathematics issue! If this court had 100 people, 100 judges, its group size error will be much lower, but great error still comes from the its Simple Majority System, unless the vote support percent is high.

A coin toss experiment to determine the fairness of a coin with HEAD and TAIL if composed of only three tosses gives no confidence in the result, because all 3 tosses may come up Head, and you can mistakenly make the decision that this coin has a probability of 100% that every toss will land Head. But you know that is not true! Even if you toss it 9 times, sometimes you may get 9 Heads, and this is less likely but possible. So do hurry to make the decision that this coin has a probability of 100% landing Head? But you know that is not likely true. Your feeling tells you, to be safe in deciding the coin's fairness on landing Head, I should have 100 or 1000 tosses, and average them, and then, and only then, I can feel comfortable about judging the fairness of this coin.

A 100 coin toss experiment for our purpose in voting computation, is similar to 100 identical coins tossed one time, or one hundred judges on a jury or 100 congressmen questioned one time YES or NO in a vote.

This mathematical similarity is extremely important because it opens the door to examine voting in a mathematical way familiar to statisticians. As of the year 2020, man has gone to outer space with advanced mathematics, yet remains in the stone age or dark ages regarding mathematics used for voting, be it math for a law making institution or public elections, mathematics which is nonexistent or incomplete, yet this is the most public arena to use mathematics on, the public square, the center of political life.

Regarding the sample size factor, here are some mathematical notes that you can skip over as technical but should be mentioned briefly:

1. For the number of people in the Congress, parliament, city hall, or company board directors, etc.: If we were to discount these people's intelligence level as a factor, a good assumption because they sometimes disagree and we do not know which group has more intelligence if any, this model becomes similar to a "fair coin toss model" for voting, and use the Central Limit Theorem and associated factors, such as Standard Deviation, and Standard Error, etc. then the sample size we use determines how much general error there is associated with this group. I will call this Standard Error Of The Mean for clarity the "**Organization Size Additional Error Rate**". This Organization Size Additional Error Rate is the same amount for every group vote, and is in addition to the error of the specific vote under consideration. So for example, the U.S.A. Congress has a specific Organization Additional Error Rate number associated with it, as does the British parliament, as does the Lebanese or Indian or Italian parliaments. Ignore this math if you want, but the formula is for a specific sample size = sqrt(p * (1 - p)/n), where p is the probability of heads or YES and is 0.5, and n is the sample size or group size. The formula reduces to **Organization Size Additional Error Rate = $\frac{0.5}{\sqrt{n}}$**

2.   Here are some examples:

a. Example 1: Senate or parliament has 100 members in it. This number results in an "Organization Size Additional Error Rate" = $\frac{0.5}{\sqrt{100}}$ = **5%** regardless of the future vote they will take. This error rate is independent of other factors and is in addition to the error that will be produced when they take a specific vote. Therefore, if the USA senate has 100 members, then it has a built in **MINIMUM** error rate of 5%, which means, regardless of the vote result, the maximum accuracy the USA Senate can have is 95%. The error is when they vote unanimously. But if they vote 80% Yes to 20% No, the 80% - 20% = 60% regular Vote Accuracy to which we subtract the **Organization Size Additional Error Rate of 5%, to become 55% accuracy. Actually, for technical reasons, we have to subtract 2 times the Organization Size Additional Error Rate amount, which means Accuracy = 60% - 2x 5% = 50%. Therefore, an 80% Yes to 20% No vote by 100 members has only 50% Quality or accuracy.**

b. Example 2: Congress or parliament has 1000 members in it. This number of people by formula results in an Organization Size Additional Error Rate = $\dfrac{0.5}{\sqrt{1000}}$ = **1.6%** associated with it regardless of the vote.

c. Example 3: Congress or parliament has 10000 members in it. The Organization Size Additional Error Rate is 0.5%.

You can see that for organizations with a large number of members, we can ignore this error factor, and remove it from calculations because it becomes too small. But for small organizations, it is very significant and should remain. For example:

d. Courts (such as the U.S.A. Supreme Court) or a board of directors in a company that has 9 members in it. The Organization Size Additional Error Rate = $\dfrac{0.5}{\sqrt{9}}$ = **17%.** Imagine this error number for a court or Supreme Court! This is the MINIMUM error, that occurs of the vote is unanimous. And since this error number has to be multiplied by two, the actual MINIMUM error in any USA Supreme Court Decision is 34%. This happens if the vote is unanimous. But the error is typically much higher because the votes are seldom unanimous. Imagine this reality, or should I say, this nightmare of justice and decision accuracy. We will use this number later in an example.

It is extremely important to understand that:

The organization size error is the minimum error and therefore it sets a maximum accuracy level for a voting group. The error is typically much higher.

This means, a voting group cannot be more accurate than its size allows! If it is a small group, its accuracy will be small. So if the Supreme Court has 9 members only, then its accuracy cannot exceed 83%! If the Senate has 100 members, then its accuracy cannot exceed 95%! Their accuracy is always lower than this. This is a very dramatic mathematical result. A judge or a politician can spend a long time thinking about the implications of just this one fact.

This statistical formula seems logical on the face of it. It basically says, **the more people are involved in a vote, the more accurate the results are likely to be**, or saying it differently, the less error is likely to be, and this minimal error cannot be eliminated. It is a mathematical reality of statistics. This is distressing when you talk about serious laws, and life and death issues because every 1% of additional error can be significant to consider.

Now, to illustrate this from real life examples, it is good to ask, would you go out driving your car, or be driven by someone who has an 80% accuracy level that he will not get into an accident? I think not, because this means that 20% of the time driving he will be involved in accidents. Some car drivers go their entire life without having a single car accident, and many may have at most one or two accidents. Can you imagine how many accidents a car driver will have at 80% accuracy, with the flipside of this being a 20 percent error rate? Will he have 1 accident per day or per week? Very possible. So while an 80% vote, or 80% accuracy seems reassuring in a vote in congress, as a result of poor awareness of the mathematics of decision making, it is an extremely low level of accuracy to accept for important decisions. In matters of law, serious family issues, or judicial issues, we want to be certain of the advice before we feel comfortable and secure in proceeding. So when I say 80%

accuracy is low, now you can understand why. A minimum of 95% accuracy may be required, and higher accuracy is better. Imagine doing a glaucoma eye surgery by three different doctors with 80%, 95%, and 99% chance of success or accuracy, correspondingly. These same numbers mean 20% chance of failure or blindness, or 5% or 1% chance of blindness in the operation. Even at 1% chance of going blind can give you much pause, because of the serious consequences of failure or error. Laws and advice can involve very serious consequences to people, so how the hell can we and have been accepting for generations votes in law chambers having accuracy of 1%, 10%, or 20% etc. These ill-educated people, including you and me probably until recently, have accepted such lunatic reality. It is lunatic, because when you put these actions to the rigor of very simple mathematical analysis, you see that we have been committing a major tragedy in error against ourselves and others. **We have been accepting what should be absolutely unacceptable**. In other words, it looks like it is one of these rare times in history that calls for an immediate and quick and radical change. Same as when people realized after thousands of years that: the earth is not flat, but is round! It was a radical change in thinking.

It is like a rocket designed to go to the moon, or a cooking recipe. All ingredients and processes have to be right, because if one ingredient or step is bad, it can be a total failure.

Example: You have to cook a potato recipe for your lunch or for your restaurant. The simple recipe calls for potatoes, tomato sauce, a dash of salt, dash of garlic powder and onion powder. What happens if the potatoes are only 70%, or 80%, or 90%, or 99% good? What will the food be like to taste and eat at each level of confidence? And now, we have to consider this question for every single ingredient in the recipe. Can you accept a 70% or 80% or 90% quality of tomato sauce, and for the garlic and onion? Now let us say you are willing to compromise on quality because you are very poor, and accept an 80% quality for each ingredient. Do you know what the total quality of the recipe is now? To compute this, you simply multiply all the qualities together. I will teach later more about this. But very simply, multiply the quality of the potatoes by the quality of the tomato sauce etc. Let use assume the quality of the salt, garlic and onion powders are 100%. So 80% multiplied by 80% by 80% by 100% by 100% by 100% results in 51% Total quality for the recipe. It should seem logical that the more bad quality ingredients you put in your recipe the worse the results will get. You may get away with one or two poor quality ingredients, but more than this, and the recipe may start to taste bad or may become unhealthy. Now the recipe involves ingredients and cooking steps. So looking at the process steps, which are cooking temperature, cooking time, amount or ratio of each ingredient, and measure the quality of each step, then we face the same process in calculating the quality. So if the recipe calls for cooking these ingredients for one hour and you cook it for only five minutes, the potatoes may still be uncooked and not edible. This step quality may have the value of 20% or possibly 0%. The recipe may call for cooking temperature to be 100 degrees, but you cook it at 50 degrees, then this quality may be valued at 60%. Now if we combine the processing steps qualities to the 51% quality recipe, then the result can become even lower. You may eat a recipe that is 51% quality or accuracy or 30% quality or accuracy and may not care about the taste or if you will die from it, but will you serve it in a restaurant? Can your restaurant succeed with such accuracy of product choice accuracy and cooking steps accuracy? Or do you want the ingredients to have 100 percent quality, 100 percent accuracy in the product selection? Do you want the cooking steps of time and temperature to be 100 percent accurate? Do you want the amount of salt to be perfect, or be ten times more and ruin the taste? For this recipe to taste great, every ingredient and cooking step has to be nearly perfect, and near 100% in accuracy. Now imagine cooking or should I say building a space ship. With one thousand ingredients and one thousand steps. Can you imagine the accuracy that is required from each component and processing step? What if any one ingredient or step is low accuracy, is it possible that it will ruin the entire space ship and make unacceptably dangerous and thus useless and a waste of money? Can you imagine a computer chip with one million ingredients or transistors, and one thousand operating processes? What is the acceptable error rate for this single chip? 1% which is 1 error in 100 part or step, or 1 error in 1000 or 1 error in one million? For some of these products, if the error rate is bigger than one on one million, the chip may not function, and your cell phone may not. Such incredibly small error rates can be considered by some electronics manufacturers as unacceptable and high. They build their products based on pure physics and mathematics. There is no guessing involved. You either know what you are doing exactly or you do not.

From all this, You should begin to understand that law makers for years have been cooking and serving us shit to eat, and we have been eating it, many happily. They neither knew what they were cooking, and did not measure accuracy using mathematics, and we never ate anything else to know the difference, and to know that we have been eating shit. It should be said in fairness that they too did not know that they are serving us shit to eat.

2nd Factor

When a vote is made on a decision, the decision must be for a singular subject or issue that cannot be broken down into smaller subjects or issues (components). This helps minimize the error in the vote decision.

Example:

If the proposed law or proposed decision is "Do task A and task B" the vote would be broken into two votes, a vote on "Do Task A" and a separate vote on "Do Task B". To understand the mathematical consequences of this action, we compute the accuracy of vote 1 and the accuracy of vote 2 separately, and the accuracy of the decision if the vote was not separated: the accuracy of the unseparated decision is the accuracy of vote 1 "multiplied" by the accuracy of vote 2.

Example:

Accuracy of vote 1 = 50% (in mathematics, 50% = 0.5, 50 out of 100 which equals half)

and

Accuracy of vote 2 = 30% (in mathematics, 30% = 0.3, 30 out of 100 which equals about a third)

To calculate the combined reliability of two items connected serially, or probability or Accuracy, you multiply their two percentages. This produces a number that is equal or smaller than either number!

So the accuracy of a combined decision is: accuracy 1 multiplied by accuracy 2 = 0.5 multiplied by 0.3 = 0.15. Which is 15%. So the accuracy of the vote on "Do task A and task B" is 15%. A lower accuracy than the accuracy gained by voting on each item separately. The mathematics is that of probability or reliability theory mathematics. Two events connected together serially, the chance of both of them happening together is the probability of the first multiplied by the probability of the second. The reliability of a system composed of two parts connected serially is the reliability of the first part multiplied by reliability of the second part which gives an equal or a lower reliability for the entire system then either part. Therefore the reason to separate every vote to the smallest component of the decision is to get the most accurate calculation of the accuracy.

Examples to understand reliability and or probability computations which for simplicity can be used interchangeably sometimes:

1. A heart doctor has 60% success rate in doing artificial heart implantation using his skills alone. His reliability therefore is 60%. He succeeds 6 times out of 10 operations or 60 times out of 100 operations. A newly invented mechanical heart device has its own separate 40% success rate in operating effectively in the long run according to the manufacturer. Therefore, the device reliability is 40%, meaning only 4 out of 10 devices are good, or meaning 6 out of 10 devices break after a short period. So the question is: what is the total reliability of this heart operation (combined reliability of the doctor and the device)? Mathematically, it is the reliability of the first multiplied by

the reliability of the second = 60% × 40% = 24%!!! The reliability or chance of success for this operation is only 24%. Very low chance of success. Very low reliability. And if it was a voting decision, we can say very low accuracy! You probably should not do this operation with this particular doctor and particular device, and similarly, you should reject accepting a vote on a law with this result.

2. The senate passes a law with 60% Accuracy. The judges on Supreme Court vote on a criminal or civil case related to this law with a vote carrying 70% Accuracy. The person in the court facing judgement is thus freed, convicted or ruled against by a total accuracy of = 60% × 70% = 42% accuracy! This person can lose his life, or his property, or his rights based on a judicial vote that has 42% accuracy. How nice! But to compute a more accurate Accuracy, we need to use the more accurate accuracy formula that accounts for the Organization size Additional error rate. So (60% * U.S.A. Senate Organization size Additional error rate of 95%) * (U.S.A. Supreme Court Organization size Additional error rate of 83% * 70%) = 33% Accuracy!!!! This man or woman or child is being judged by a process that has 33% accuracy or confidence. Note: I am simplifying by considering only the senate chamber which has 100 members, and leaving out the other chamber, but the numbers are very telling, and seem unreal.

3. Are you beginning to understand the mathematics and its consequences? This does not even consider if the law content is fundamentally sound! This is simply the voting process mathematics on the best wisdom (guess) of congress on an issue combined with the best wisdom (guess) of judges. **For group guessing, there is a science and this is the mathematics. This is the shocking reality and tragic consequences of ignorance.**

3rd Factor

It is important to give greater consideration (weight) to those voting NO than to those voting YES. In some areas in life, it is similar to the principle of "First, Do No Harm" as supposedly is the case in medicine. Or it is similar to the subject of "Risk Aversion" where bigger weight is given to harm than to benefits. For example, if 50% of people say take this particular medicine because it has harmless side effects, and another 50% tell you do not take it because it may cause you death immediately, will you give both groups' advice equal weight? Most likely no, because of the seriousness of the consequences. The greater the damage is from a wrong decision, the more weight we give the NO vote. Even if it was 90% telling you take the medicine, and only 10% saying NO because you will die, you may give the 10% NO votes a much higher weight than to the 90% saying YES and decide not to risk taking this medicine. Therefore we must guard much more against the damage (consequences) done to people who are objecting to the vote, because the harm done to them maybe much higher than the benefits gained by those who favour the vote. And we may not know the value or consequences (or how to compute them) of the vote to every particular bystander citizen. How do you compute the value (price) of freedom for an individual, when one person may give it no value while another be willing to lose his life for it? It is like voting on a law for death penalty and we should give greater weight to those who say No to the decision because of the seriousness and the damage and irreversibility of the damage done to a person effected by this law. If he loses his life because of an erroneous decision, found out later, how do you restore back his life, and how do you compensate his family? What do you tell his family?

An example of how to solve this mathematically is by biasing the formula to give two times or three times more weight to the opposing group, etc. But we will **keep it very simple, so that the math is clear, sharp, adequate, and can be understood easily by many, and applied easily in town halls, city halls and parliaments and congresses because this issue is so serious and effects all of us, billions of human beings.**

Realistic and typical example to parliaments or congresses to show the magnitude of their errors, and how the mathematics works.

Let us say there is a country that has a parliament or a congress that is in charge of making laws. One congressman, call him congressman A, proposes a law that confiscate 10 percent of every citizen's income to give to the poor who have no money. Let us call this is law A. This congressman finds out that 30 percent of congressman will support him which, is not enough to cross the 51 percent required to become a law. Another congressman we will call him congressman B has a law, we will call it law B, which will force a close down of government and business for an official holiday he declares as "Intelligence Day" which he hopes will makes citizens aware of the importance of intelligence. Congressman B finds out only 30 percent of congressman will support him for that, which means his law will not pass. Both laws seem very bad and each has no accuracy, zero accuracy (negative accuracy).

Congressman A and congressman B get together and agree with each other saying support my law and I will support your law, and this way your 30 percent support and my 30 percent support will make give 60 percent support if we combine our two laws under 1 vote. The congress votes on the combined bill composed of law A and law B and law A and law B pass and become law by the support of 60 percent vote. The combination of law A and law B we will call law C.

Let us compute the accuracy of Law C.

Accuracy of law C = 60% (yes) - 40% (no) = 20% accuracy. Law C now has some accuracy, when it should have none. It should have zero accuracy. This again illustrates why it should not be allowed to combine laws in a vote. It shows how proposed laws that have absolutely no accuracy (zero accuracy) can become law easily. Now imagine a typical congress or parliament single vote on a single bill containing 100 laws or 1000 laws. Is this real? Are you beginning to understand the magnitude of the error and the gravity of the problem. This example illustrates:

1. How laws in practice are made and how flawed the process of law making can be.
2. It illustrates how to compute the accuracy of a law.
3. It illustrates how combining laws has a disastrous effect on the accuracy of decisions. Laws that have no accuracy when combined together can achieve one law that has very big accuracy, which is very misleading, because it is a corruption of a proper voting process.
4. It illustrates **the absolute importance and necessity for the concept that every vote must be broken to the smallest component of the law proposed.** That is, law C would be forced to be

broken down into its components, in this case, component A and component B and each be voted on separately, and law A and law B would not pass and neither would law C. And citizens would be spared such stupid laws and such stupid law process and law makers and this tragedy imposed on almost every citizen on earth.

5. One important aside: A law has to be used in the court by a judge or a jury. We saw how laws are passed with low accuracy or even when passed with high accuracy still have risk about their correctness. A judge or a jury also have to vote on a decision and their voting process also needs to have calculation for accuracy. The tragedy of errors becomes even greater because now we are combining the low confidence in the correctness of the law with the uncertain correctness of the judge or jury vote. Therefore if a law passes by accuracy of 80 percent and a jury votes has accuracy of 60 percent then the combined accuracy is 80 percent multiplies by 60 percent = 48 percent, which is a low level to use in court to judge the affairs of man. If you can really understand this and the consequences on freedom, on decision making accuracy, on oppression, you will begin to appreciate how tragic human beings' situation is all over the world, by being so much less than what it can be.

It is extremely important before considering a law to ask these questions: Is it an absolute necessity? Do we know how to compute the cost-benefit factors involved? Is it of a great urgency to deal with security or criminal issues? Or is it a matter of civilian nature? If it is a matter of civil nature, the law makers would be wise to not touch or involve themselves in such issues. If it is a security or criminal issue then the law makers should be well versed in the accuracy of the law so they can make the best decision possible. Your ignorance is our tragedy.

And **if "ignorance of the law cannot be a defense in court, and an innocent person is made a criminal and is imprisoned", when a lawmaker or a judge is ignorant of the mathematics of voting and decisions and the law making process, can he claim ignorance as a defense? Can he be safe from a higher judgement to be made a criminal? A criminal against men stemming from his ignorance? If he is afforded rights of ignorance, should not an accused be afforded the same rights?**

Criminals may use a weapon to overpower another human being to commit a crime", while law makers use "the law" to overpower a human being to commit a crime. Both are equally guilty and both are criminals. The first criminal often causes injury to one or few humans, while the second criminal often causes injury to millions of humans at the same time. The second criminal and his supporters seem to have no understanding of his crimes, and their enormous magnitude. The first criminal is usually punished while the second criminal is free from criminal punishment and is often celebrated by many for his crimes.

Few formulas as "The Accuracy Of The Vote" when understood and used properly will affect the life of man for the better as this.

Qualifications for a law maker

Questions to ask yourself if you are considering to enter politics and become a law maker:

1. Do you know basic mathematics, specifically, basic algebra and basic probability theory and its related "decision theory mathematics"? If designing airplanes, high rise buildings, computers and cell phones is base on mathematics and physics in order not to cause injury and to function properly then, this minimal understanding of mathematics is necessary for accurate decision making.
2. Are you seeking political office and law making to give rights to one group by taking away from the rights of another group?
3. Are you aiming to give money and new programs to one group by confiscating the money of another group?
4. Are you physically and mentally a well abled individual with a varied life experience that does not aim to fix a personal shortcoming or inabilities at the expense of others who have well being?

Qualifications of citizens to elect a law maker

It is not far fetched to expect many citizens' votes during elections to not be of high accuracy, because they lack basic knowledge of mathematics and probability theory and its effect in decision making. It may be completely inappropriate to put any qualifications on adult citizens being able to vote, such as requiring this knowledge. Therefore, it seems wise that when law makers get to office, they can limit themselves, by requiring future law makers coming into office be elected by votes that have high accuracy. No longer can politicians be elected by winning 51% or 60% or even 70% of the votes! These offices will be empty, and there is nothing wrong with this. However, since the government needs some administrators or overseers, other solutions can be readily found.

Qualifications of universities to teach politics and law

As of today, I would venture to guess that every university that has a department for teaching politics have their department named as "Political Science department". But a better name for these departments may be "Political Arts Department" or "Political Philosophy Department". Using the word science in a name implies use of the precision of mathematics and mathematical tools in the field, where the entire subject, from A to Z is taught based on mathematics. That is not the case now. Not by any stretch of the imagination. Change it. (Update May 30, 2021: I have risen to the challenge and wrote the book "A Mathematical Foundation For Politics And Law" as a text book).

Here is a section from the book "Jamil" modified and cuss words added because of the incredible importance of this subject and how much damage is being done by uneducated and unresponsive people and lawmakers (similar to a situation with a house on fire with young children who do not understand yet to run out or do something) :

The Index Of Social Intelligence:

Best is the simplest version: The government shall make no civil laws, without the explicit consent of every citizen (100 percent) approval. In other words, it is better not to make any civil laws.
Violating this principle can be a violation of an individual's rights, and if this individual takes it upon himself to remedy the situation, I don't know if he can be blamed.
But to expand and make clear, here is a breakdown of what this can mean, basic freedoms that should be preserved and can serve as an indication of some intelligence in a society and culture:

- The freedom to self defence. Clearly this means the right to own and carry the tools to do it, otherwise it is meaningless. So owning of firearms and carrying it concealed or not, is a right

- The freedom to eat whatever I want. It is my body, you bastard uneducated shit

- The freedom to drink whatever I want. It is my body, you bastard uneducated shit

- The freedom to inhale/smoke whatever I want. It is my body, you bastard uneducated shit

- The freedom to put in my body whatever I want. It is my body, you bastard uneducated shit

- The freedom to say whatever I want. If you don't like it, don't read it. Change the channel. You bastard ignorant uneducated shit

- The freedom to think whatever I want, and to have unrestricted access to read, and listen without interference

- The freedom to believe whatever I want and practice it. (Naturally, if it does not infringe on you)

- The right to give my money or property to who ever I want, and to give as much of it as I want, at any time. This means also in public elections

- The freedom to dress however I want or not to dress at all, the freedom for nudity in public. (Few things human beings can do, that will benefit them as the practice of public nudity. I cannot stress enough its importance.)

- The freedom to have sex between consenting adults, even if for money

- The freedom to gamble

- The freedom to travel

- The freedom to decide the amount of risk I am willing to accept in any event or action I undertake. The government has no right to interfere in this. Life is full of risks of every sort, physical, financial, business, products, social etc. (The government cannot interfere under the guise of protecting the citizen or consumer or worker etc.)

- The freedom to lend money for interest. Lending of money is a consensual civil act, and failure to have the debt repaid is a risk the lender takes. It is not proper for the lender or borrower to bind the government (society, everyone in it including you and me) into such private contracts when there are defaults on contracts. Do not make me, or cost me, to be a party in your private contracts.

- The freedom to associate with only people or groups of your choice, to discriminate. A discriminating person is an intelligent person. Discrimination is an essential part of intelligence and of freedom of choice. The uneducated or evil have made discrimination a social taboo, and is even considered a crime in some societies, by creation of such terms as "hate crime" etc.

- The freedom to not have your money confiscated by government by force of gun or by tax laws (both are theft). "Use-cost fees" seem like a possible solution. (Note: Taxation is typically the oxygen that can strengthen and feeds the enemy of freedom, a bad or big government). Learn and create intelligent private ways for meet large projects funding if desired

- The freedom to have a national identity card, that cannot be taken / stripped from you by anyone (including the government), and that can be used for travel locally and internationally

- The freedom to own your child. A child is born a property of the mother, completely as part of her physical body, as an arm or leg or hair, and then for her to decide all matters. Also, all the responsibilities are hers alone. No matter how uneducated, incapable, or irresponsible she may be, the baby is hers, and the decisions and control are completely hers: To educate or not, and how to, what they eat, drink, smoke, learn, or do, etc. No government or anyone can mandate to her. Having given a woman sperm does not constitute a person becoming a parent or obligated to be one. Also, what this means is that the father has zero obligations towards the child or the mother. Zero obligations financially or otherwise. What a father does in support is out of love. So a child born is not a financial transaction for the benefit of the mother. A social welfare system of sort to fuck the men financially. If you need money for your life, get educated and get a job or learn about birth control. The mother decides who the parents are. She or they, not the government, decide the age of child maturity. Do not allow or make the government or society play the role of a mother and father. They are not. At least do not make them mine. If you need a mother and a father to tell you what to do, go find your mother or father, or get adopted

- The freedom to birth control and to abort a pregnancy, that is, to kill the fetus. It is her body, not yours, you uneducated shit. This is redundant with her freedom to do as wish with her body or her child. I use the word "kill" to not mince words or get scared by others from words. Just as cutting your nail is killing living cells, and cutting your hair, or an ugly mole, or a cancer lump, or a kidney you cut to donate or throw away, these are all living cells or organs that are a part of your body and for no one to interfere whatsoever with what you do with it. And donating an egg, to outside her body, to give to another person, does not make her the mother or owner any longer

- The right for a man or a women or a group of them to live together as they wish without interference from religion or the government. To procreate and give each other rights as they wish. It is my strong but personal opinion that sex should be only between a man and a woman as the hygienic and natural order of a human being

- The freedom to buy and sell a product or a service, consensually, between two parties, without government interference. Clearly, this also means without restriction on day or time or age. This includes the right to hire or be hired. (Regarding children, and this is redundant right to repeat, I grew up and still live sometimes in places were it is the norm for very young children to work in their parent's stores to sell or be sent to buy alcohol or tobacco or medicine etc. It is not for anyone except the parents to decide in such issues, and for the business owner)

- The freedom to die

- The freedom from forced confinement due to attempt to suicide or mental illness problems (confinement such as in a hospital or jail)

- Freedom from business regulations; a worker or customer can go somewhere else if unhappy. The owner is not obliged to accommodate a customer or a worker or government specifications relating to the product or worker or its environment. You bastard uneducated dumb shit. Mind our own damn business! Not mine. No one is forcing you to buy it, and no one is forcing you to work here. Go the f!k somewhere else if you do not want it or like it. I am not your father or mother obliged to you. How stupid have humans become to accept or be forced to accept such shit logic!

- The freedom from governments forcing a citizen into a service. Such as military or court jury service. If a person objects to killing humans he does not know, or agree with the reason for killing, how can you force him to do it? Government service can only be voluntary

- The freedom to own private property, and the right to protect it

- The freedom from the criminalization of civil acts. Some in society will want to make civil acts to be defined as criminal acts, so **guard firmly against this**. The definition of a civil act and a criminal act should be very clearly defined. Civil advisories seem acceptable, advisories of best available knowledge of a community to help guide actions. Advisories are not mandatory and are for a common community, at a common time and place.

- Do not allow laws that convert a "private contract" by their nature, to become a "public contract". Examples of private contracts are: money lending, or a marriage agreement between two people

- The freedom from using the terms "Community standards" and "society" against the individual. Both are abstract terms and are the antithesis of freedom and should have no foundation in law as I explain. Only the individual matters and is the real entity that can represent itself and has rights. Allowing such terms and concepts as "community standards" may sound good at the surface to the uneducated but can be the death nail of personal freedom of choice. These rights outlined and spoken about in this book belong only to the individual, and not society.

- While Community Standards is a social concept, Eminent Domain is the equivalent economic concept. The first is mob power that can erase all your civil rights, and the second is mob power that can erase all your private property rights.

- Unscientific voting result computations are another deadly mob power tool to erase ALL your rights. The voter participating in a poll should know the basic Poll Accuracy equation = YES% - NO%, and those conducting the poll should know the full Poll Accuracy equation.

Guard diligently against such terms, concepts, and practice.

- The freedom from international treaties that are not in line with local laws. A treaty cannot be for a local law that does not exist. First, the law if any is created locally, then agreed to internationally, not the other way around.

- In short, the freedom from all civil laws

- It is important that you have the minimal logical ability to understand that: If you asked for advice from 100 people on how to proceed on a two option fork of the road, go left or go right? And 50% said go left and 50% said go right, then the value of this advice is zero! And, can you understand similarly that a result of 49% saying go left and 51% saying go right is almost the same and has near 0 value? And can you understand that a good advice on how to proceed should have near unanimity by those advising, or voting? If you are not able to understand this, then your logic ability and education are not sufficient for you to participate in public voting, since you are a threat to my liberty, property, money, and general well-being. The Poll Accuracy formula = YES percent - NO percent, in simple form when the number of voters in a poll is large, and a high precision Poll Accuracy formula for any group size = (YES% - NO%) - $4/\sqrt{n}$, where n is voters total size (see the mathematics book for details).

Note about **Victimless Crimes Or Acts**: Looking at the Index Of Social Intelligence, we can conclude for example that, if no laws should be enacted regarding consensual sex, but if a parliament does and bans prostitution, and a person is imprisoned for this, then this is a victimless crime. Both parties in this act agree with each other in this private contract, with all the risks involved. Same for civil issues between two parties, such as marriage or child support, or money lending. Here are more examples: Owning a weapon for self defence. Serving MSG food additives or trans fats in restaurants. Having a restaurant that allows smoking. Selling alcohol or tobacco or drugs. Speaking your mind, or writing. Driving without a helmet. Walking nude in public. Freedom of association.

Stop taking peoples' freedoms and stop wasting money on jails, police, lawyers, courts and politicians on such issues. Empty your prisons quickly from all such acts. You are aggressing against these people by putting them in jail. You are not using a gun to rob their freedoms, but using unjust and bad laws with the same effect. How can you do this? Are you so uneducated in logic and human values to understand this, even after reading these writings? You, the parliament or congress or president or the judge, are the ones committing a crime, when you do this, not these people.

- The freedom from international civil treaties, (and criminal treaties). These are or can be used to circumvent, get around, local laws. Guard diligently against this. Using such mechanisms as treaties to bind people by foreign laws that they would not accept in their local laws or know about is better be prohibited. Treaties cannot be about civil issues. (Only criminal if any, and should be in line with local standards. The problem is that another backward country can define a civil act as criminal, according to their standards, and then can make it a criminal act in your country or if you travel to their country. How nice! Here you are innocently at the airport and you get arrested for some alleged violation you are not aware of. Now spent time, money, lawyers, and bail if you can, while you try to convince some person or court in a backward or advanced country, to free yourself.) Freedom is freedom in your own country and from other countries' laws that are in cahoots with your country to take your freedom in indirect way. It is better to have associations of countries who share the same values. If you have the same laws, then you can form an organization. If local laws change, they are removed from the organization. Laws start from the ground up, not top down, preserving local power above all.

General principle: If my actions do not limit your freedom of choice, then a law for the act should not exist. Example: Free speech. If you do not like a book, newspaper, radio, or TV program, you have the option to not tune to it. So you should not create any laws that interfere in this. Same for food or food service places. If a restaurant wants to allow smoking, and you do not like smoking, you have the option not to go there. Etc. If you feel your freedom is infringed upon by having a newspaper that issues views you dislike, and it should be banned, this is not infringing on your freedom. No one is forcing you to read it. Infringing on your freedom of choice means limiting your freedom of choice. In this case, your choice has not been limited, but to the contrary, it has been expanded. Same for selling tobacco, alcohol or drugs or prostitution or parachuting or sky diving or motorcycle driving. They carry risks for the individual to decide on, and not for you, and they do not limit your choice and are not a direct physical threat to you. How does the existence of a restaurant for smokers limit your choice or does you direct physical harm? You and cows fart on occasion and that is general air pollution, and some limited pollution is inevitable, but you can get away from it. Having a restaurant for smokers increases your choice, not limits it. You may hate smoking for what ever reason, but your choices are preserved, and you can choose not to select this restaurant, just as you choose in life not to select many things you dislike. But don't take this choice from others who want it.

General principle: Do not allow laws that convert a "private contract" by their nature, to become a "public contract". Examples of private contracts are: money lending, or a marriage agreement between two people. A private contract in case of disputes should remain private and be resolved by and at cost of the private parties involved. A public contract is enforced by public courts and at the cost of the citizens, you and me, pay the cost of. The cost of courts, jails, and enforcement, all of which are an imposition on other citizens which are not parties to the dispute. Examples to make this clear:

Default on debt between lender and borrower.

A lender lending a drunk, or mentally handicapped or highly uneducated person or giving a shark-loan etc. is acting to his advantage. Some will try to insert the government into this, saying the answer is more laws that protects the mentally handicapped or drunk or uneducated etc. It is not for the government to be the judge about who is fit or not which inserts the government into the role of the enforcer. The government should not judge in private contracts nor be the enforcer. The private parties in the contract between them bear all the risks and costs or benefits. And if there is default on the loan, he should bear full responsibility in this private contract. And I should not be a party to enforcing your private contract, by allowing you to take this issue to a public court and pay for the courts or prisons or police, etc. Some things involve risk, and when you indulge in them, you should bear the total cost and benefits, not me. By the same logic, marriage should be a private and not a public contract. Do not make me a party in it when there is a problem and force me to spend for the courts etc. Resolve your private contract disputes through your own mechanisms, be it private mediators or otherwise.

General principle: The challenges. We rely on best logic as our guide in life, and assume it to be the bases for human interaction. We care about physical security against threats as a priority, such as being attacked, or physically threatened. Therefore, a proper state of mind is important in relations for us to feel secure. A person drinks alcohol or takes drugs at his house, and stays there till the effects are gone and his judgment (logic) ability is restored. I have no right to interfere in what he does. But if a person is drugged, drunk, or mentally deranged to the point of being a physical threat, then this can complicate issues, and needs to be looked at. In such cases, the mind may become incapable of making logical judgement that we expect people to have. And they can become a physical threat. So the case of "mind altering acts" should be studied carefully, to permit both, freedom of action, without it being a physical threat to others. Example: ingesting a drug, that in small quantity is relaxing, but in large quantity, may greatly effect a person's judgement (logic) on a road. It is a very difficult issue to deal with. With a gun at my side, if a person impaired of judgement attacks me or threatens me, because he is hallucinating from drug use, or from being mentally handicapped, or being a thief, I can protect myself and shoot them. That may be the best solution that protects completely my freedom and his freedom. In this case, there is a person to person encounter, and I have a chance to defend myself against normal risks in life. But if such a hallucinating person starts and drives a car while I am in another car, I have no such opportunity to defend myself because I cannot be aware of the threat oncoming. Difficult issue to deal with, but maybe good solutions can be found. Life involves many risks, and it is not the function of a stranger (government) to tell me how much risk I can have in it. This should be an individual choice. The best we can do is educate well, voluntarily, and be prepared to deal with the harm if it comes near, as an unavoidable cost of having freedom. Try to be creative in finding solutions that preserve these desires. A difficult task, but using best thinking (scientific) that preserves good values is preferable. Some will fight and die for their freedoms to be preserved and others may be willing to sell it for one dollar. How do we know which is the better value? Freedom is, because it preserves both their choices. Freedom contains both choices, while the opposite does not. Freedom allows freedom and lack of it as a personal choice, while lack of freedom, oppression, only allows oppression. Freedom can be very slow acting sometimes, and is a strong foundation to build on, while oppression can be very fast acting sometimes, and is a weak foundation to build on. Often, people's uneducated instincts under threat are to turn to quick and tried solutions that bring immediate results. But this may not be best in the long run. And sometimes, it may be wise to have guidance in short time, and then to completely remove it later, as a child under control of parent, and then completely free later to act on his own as adult. But in matters of law creation, this is difficult to emulate, because once a law is enacted, it is difficult to cancel, and difficult to know when to cancel it. When erring in matters of law making, it seems proper to err on the side of freedom. It has been said that it is wise to let one hundred guilty prisoners free, than to imprison one innocent person. Law making is a matter of values. Educate well and choose your values.

All rights not expressly given by a particular person (a person that has a name), then this specific person is exempted from this law. This is not lawlessness, because long before there were governments, people lived and managed without such needs.

I showed you how much ignorance there is in law making. So stop taking these peoples freedom and stop wasting. And when the constitution tells a law maker "Do not do this or that" and the law maker does it; what resort does the citizen have? You have just committed a crime against him. How do you put him in jail or more? If the constitution says do not make laws against free speech, and the law maker does. When the constitution says "all rights not expressly delegated by the citizen to the government do not belong to the government" and the law maker takes your rights anyway, rights to eat, drink, inhale, dress, etc. as you wish, what recourse do you have against these very high level aggressions?

Because this document is about civil freedoms, it is important to discuss very briefly the other side of the issue, to enhance clarity. **There are civil issues and criminal issues. It is extremely important to know the distinction** and to define criminal issues well, so that they will not be mistaken with civil issues. There should not be "punitive" punishment by government or courts for civil acts. Punitive means incarceration (such as jail), or any forced enforcement on his property (such as court ordered taking or seizing of property, money, or other rights). For example: in a divorce or child related issues, these are civil issues, neither party can be jailed or have their salary or property affected. The government cannot use force on either party. The government should not even be involved. The child is the mother's and completely hers and her responsibility. Unless physically harmed, a criminal issue, the government has no role.

I may not have an excellent or complete definition of "a criminal act", but I will give you a good starting **definition. A criminal act is a direct intent to act or threat of literal physical injury to a person or to take away basic freedom by physical force or take or injure their property. As part of the definition, there are always two components present: intent, and use of physical force.** Court **punitive action can only be for a criminal act**. Lastly, there should be a presumption of innocence for an accused, because almost any person can make or make up an accusation against another person.

So a definition of a Civil Issue is:

Civil Issue is what is not a Criminal Issue

Parents disputes, child support issues disputes, business contracts disputes, etc. are not criminal issues. It has become fashionable to make some of these civil acts criminal because of lobbying power of some groups, financial interests, or societal ignorance or through international treaties. There is a tendency for many groups to feel that they should obtain what they think as their rights in any way, including making the non criminal violation of their civil rights a criminal act. Do not allow this to happen.

The right to trial by jury and the nullification of law by the jury: that is, make the law inapplicable or useless. In a criminal act, a jury can decide to ignore the law, because the law sometimes can be incomplete, incorrect, or not applicable to the particular situation, or to override a bad judge.

The freedom to take the law into your own hands. Most times, there are no government security forces around you, so if there is a criminal act being committed in front of you, such as your old neighbor being attacked or crying for help, you can arrest or shoot the attacker, as proper action.

(Note: Fear is an oxygen that feeds the need for government. Fears of different types: imagined fear (created by media or gossip), exaggerated, or intentionally created to cause call for government, or poor solutions suggested to problems, or poorly educated public).

Lastly, all this is immaterial if your children and adults do not learn these values well, practice them, and commemorate them.

So maybe a good constitution for a town or country would be: This is the definition of what a civil act is and a criminal act is "We do not allow civil laws to be created, people do what they choose that makes them happy, and as for criminal laws we have none, and it is wise to be civil and not to do a crime because someone may harm you back or kill you."

It is absolutely remarkable that these minimal and basic freedoms seem to be lacking everywhere on earth. Even the supposedly advanced societies on earth are great violators of these freedoms as of this publication date.

I do not know how these societies or cultures can call themselves intelligent, because these freedoms seem to be the minimum required before the thought process in a human being can begin to take place unrestricted.

The more absent these freedoms are from society the less intelligent the society is likely to be. Freedom is one of the most essential ingredients needed for a society to be intelligent socially, economically and in other spheres. It is an essential component for economic success.
Freedom does not guarantee success, but without it you are less likely to have optimal success.
If the foundation of engineering, that creates useful products, is physics, with its math equations, then politics, culture and economics are the engineering that should be built on these freedom equations as foundation. When you observe these principles, laws become extremely few and relating only to criminal law, which in turn also can disappear. And lawmakers and politicians may find little work if any to do, becoming mediators and private contract makers.
To learn more, and how bad laws are, and how they are made, read my book "Creating Freedom On Earth".

In the discussion of law and freedom, it is important to understand these principles :

1. The law is to serve man, and not for man to serve the law. And if law cannot do this, remove it.

2. The word "society" is an abstraction. While the word "individual" is concrete. An individual is an identifiable specific person with a name, age, etc. His rights or grievances are all that matters for the law. And his rights or grievances can be only against a specific person or specific group of individually identifiable persons involved in the grievance (not society in the abstract or in general). With this, expanded on greatly in concrete logic, we can reach the conclusion that laws should only deal with grievances between individuals only, and there are no bases for granting society any rights in the law. Society has no rights. Only the individual has rights.

3. These rights are his, not given by others. What he chooses to relinquish of his rights to others, he cannot use as imposition on others. So if you do not like to drink alcohol and are willing to relinquish

this right, you have no right to force others to do the same. That is, do not force a ban of alcohol just because you do not want it for yourself.

4. Every law may be an unwanted imposition on another individual. And therefore, laws can have extremely high cost to some, costs you have no right to impose on them.

5. The underlying process of law making and law adjudicating should be founded on science build purely on mathematics. I have laid the foundation to do so in my books.

In life, in general, give preferences to people who you like and share your values, in your personal affairs and business affairs. For example, when you buy a product or a service it seems wise to buy these from people you would like to see become more successful. This is how you make yourself stronger in some areas that relate to values, culture, or politics. This way, your values hopefully win against the other people who oppose your values. I cannot tell you how difficult psychologically for me to practice this value, when I stopped buying from many shops that looked like they belong to persons from religions that oppose my values, and others for similar reasons. If I was able to buy the product or service from another place, then I did, and sometimes, when even when the price was higher. Your actions have consequences in the short term and the long term that affect you and affects others, and you have to decide the price of your own values, and at what cost you will sell them. If this index becomes a reality, it will be a major transformation for better on earth. Make it a reality.

More from the book "Jamil" on few of the motivations and groups that drive creation of laws:

The psychologies of the weak, ugly, evil, or uneducated, sometimes can be harmful

Educate humans against acquiring the mentality of the weak, ugly (the "unattractive" as maybe more polite word to use), evil, or uneducated. These mentalities create problems for the individual, and for the society. Weak people may have tendencies to cluster around friends, within groups, and in politics to leech off other people or weaken the strong. They will use social acts, politics, or the law to restrict them, tax them, take away their money, and affect their social standing, because they envy them, or their successes, or feel entitled to benefits or things forcefully paid for by others. Educate people to be aware of this and for them to guard against it and such tendencies.

Form a united front against such groups to protect yourself and your interests. Educate the weak not weaken the strong just because they can, by aggregating. Educate the strong not to attack the weak, just because they are able. Develop group techniques and teach these methods from childhood. It creates a more peaceful society with citizens growing up and living with a greater level of serenity and sense of security, with freedom fully preserved. Even though life may put you in a weak spot at times, it is better to adopt good principles and not let yourself be swayed by your circumstance. Awareness of the challenge helps you overcome it.
Learning to deal with all these factors creates a better individual.
Spread the principle "control yourself, not others. Use your own money, not others. (Tax yourself, not others)."
End of quotation

Example of how the psychology of the weak causes wrong behavior:
In the Index Of Social Intelligence, the first right I speak of is the right for self defense. It seems that nothing could be more important and logical than this right. It also means owning weapons if a person wants to. Yet, few things evoke as much fear for the so-called "advanced societies" or others as this right. Uniformly as of my recent knowledge, they do not allow this right. And if allowed, this right is limited.

The fear of many citizens is of someone walking with a gun, thinking they can shoot anyone at will. They have forgotten that not too long ago, this was the natural practice for many, to walk with a gun or a sword before that. And they forgot that if everyone carried a gun, the psychology and culture quickly changes to adapt, and a possible offender will also modify his thinking, and will not offend more than todays' gangsters and criminals.

Focusing on how the psychology of the weak plays a role, I will use the example of the group of "women" who in general are physically weaker than men. This causes inherent psychological fear of being attacked by a stronger man and causes them to want the existence of police or government institutions that provide security. They become advocates of laws and bigger government in its involvement in human relations. If women were educated properly, I would expect them to be strongest supporters of freedom to own a gun and carry it. Women in general today have not yet reached the understanding and psychological comfort of the extremely important idea that "a very small gun in their pocket or purse can neutralize the strongest man in seconds! And provide ready safety when they are well trained to use it, providing much of the needed security in any location." And today, guns can have a light, like a laser flashlight, to aim the bullet, making the use of such gun extremely accurate, quick, and fast to aim. Just raise it, look at the light to aim, and shoot. Even in minutes you can learn to use such a gun. So keep one on your side, or in pocket or purse if you want. With this simple reality, a woman elevates her security and strength and freedom to that of any man. In a quick draw of the gun, a criminal or an offending person is shot, and this balances the equation of physical power. What more could you want? Why are you not demanding such freedom for yourself. The reason is ignorance or bad logic brought about by adopting the psychology of the weak from early on in life. Women generally have smaller physical strength than men and gentler personality, both are qualities many prefer as feminine, and this should not be a reason for them to have less security or freedom than men in a civil or uncivil society.

Freedom of choice is not likely to be diminished when a person is surrounded by civil, intelligent, math-and-logic knowing persons. But this environment is not easy to find sometimes, and as such, the smallest bully or group of gangsters or a large group can take away a person's complete freedom of choice. Under such circumstance, the power of a gun on a person's side is the best protection of such freedom. Therefore to protect your freedom from bullies, you MUST be willing to use a gun and to kill. Not having this will, may easily cause your freedom to be taken away.

Just a touch on the psychologies of some law makers, politicians and the like:
The Law maker: A person that is extremely dangerous to your liberty and property. He is armed with great intentions of helping you. He is a stranger to you, but he wants to tell you what to eat, drink, dress, how to run your company, what wages you must accept if you need a job, he wants to give you so many gifts of health care, education, social security and programs, but he does not pay for it out of his own pocket, and confiscates the money from someone else to gift it to you. He insists that a program to be good, it must be a forced official government program, not a private or voluntarily developed program. He believes he knows your interests better than you do, and he is not your father or your mother and you are an adult, but he can make you do things, because he is armed not with a gun, where it is easy to understand the situation and the problem, instead, he is armed with a powerful tool that is called the law. A law that he and others like him create and enact on

you or me despite my objection. He is also armed with great ignorance, about mathematics, and the mathematics of decision making and its consequences on my freedom and life. Ignorant of the mathematics of cost and benefit. Ignorant of the price of freedom. In short he is armed with ignorance and armed with considering himself a do-gooder, a deadly combination to combat. Combine this with ignorant citizens neighbours, citizens who feel they are do-gooders, and the situation becomes a total nightmare. That is our situation today, a nightmare, a tragedy on a massive scale. Jails full of people involved in victimless crimes that should be let free immediately, and a bigger jail has been created for the almost all, the knowing and the unknowing.

And knowing what lawmakers all over the world have done and continue to do to billions of human beings, the author stacked all the pictures of parliaments and congresses he had and took his shotgun, aimed and blew them up, not. But, that is what he felt like doing. Others may actually act on this feeling, if the mathematics is correct, the lawmaker knows it, and does not implement it. After all, are you ignorant of this mathematics or are you evil? Some want to rule by force of gun or force of law, and if that is what you want, some citizen or a group of them may choose to give you what you like, and they may choose the force of gun.

The End.

Some notes follows:

A side note:

Criminal law:

I do not want to write much about criminal law beyond few more simple general principles for education purpose, because we are stuck with the fact the we come into this world not from the beginning of when laws are built, but from the middle, and our effort is to fix or better and more difficult, to tear down laws or the law. I am dealing with both sides of the issue. Briefly and without much elaboration:

- **A jury of judges or people is better than one judge**. Since in grave matter in law courts, such as supreme courts, or judging a president, it has been regarded as wise to have multiple judges. This practice is an indirect admission or is inherent recognition that a single judge can make mistakes, and by having multiple judges, the possibility of error is reduced, therefore it seems wise mathematically to improve a judging decision by use of a jury of judges or people. The Qur'an Islamic religious book advices something like 3 or 4 judges in some issues as a wise. The U.S.A. Supreme court has 9 judges. The trial of Socrates had about 500 jurors. Different courts have different numbers of judges or jurors, but none of these seem to give a mathematical foundation for choosing the number. It seems arbitrary or traditional with no "statistical confidence formula" used to specify why the number they chose provides a pre-specified accuracy or confidence level for the system they use. If this is an expensive process, and if human justice is the goal, then that is a part of the price. And, if you cannot do justice properly, then it may be best not to do it at all, because a very high price will be paid by the victim or accused. There is not continuous mathematical curve drawn for justice between mediocre justice and excellent justice. Justice means excellence, without deviation. And if justice is too expensive to pay for to be achieved, it may be better not done and the issue left to resolve itself by other means, primarily for the victim and accused to resolve it amicably or not and privately or not. A Non Partisan Citizen Has No Obligation To Provide To Others The Cost Of Justice.
- **The Parties Involved In A Criminal Dispute Bear The Responsibility And Right To Make The Error In Settlement, And Not The Public**. I as a nonpartisan citizen in this conflict refuse to be made a party to using laws I know are inherently flawed and a process that is inherently flawed.
- **Justice properly done means accepting the reality that many disputes cannot be resolved in court**
- As the person harmed, he has the full right to:
1. Cancel the application of the law, which means he does not want government interference in his grievance.
2. Cancel the judge's final ruling completely or partially as he pleases (lessening the punishment if any is given).
3. Settle with the accused without any outside interference.

Values are very important and come from culture or parents or religion, etc. In some countries. If you steal they'll cut your hand. Other places may put you in prison mandatory and other places may leave it to the judge or the jury and others may simply shoot you as a personal option for settlement. It can all be considered valid. Some religions give you different values. Some say as Jesus did: **forgive them because they do not know what they do**, or **he who is without sin let him cast the first stone**. These are completely different values than cutting hands or hanging etc. Jesus also said **settle your differences quickly and outside the court**. But how many Christian dominated countries practice these values????? I want to suggest a value very strongly as a guide to solving disputes, and that the first principle is it should be up to the supposed victim in a crime and the accused to resolve their situation privately or with help of parents. Requesting as part of a private settlement that the offender get the required education to learn of their error and be tested that they understand this is an interesting private resolution concept, for the victim to feel the offense will not happen again. **My value is "give people what they like, if they like violence and harm, give it to them, and if they like forgiveness, civility and education, give it to them."**

It seems proper to ask each family: If your father or son or daughter committed a crime, what would be a good punishment? Empathy, a foundation of some human relations, may be a guide in private settlement or court, with each family playing the opposite role, where the family of the victim can play the role of the family of the accused and vice versa.

Or to bring the issues to rigorous mathematical solutions, use game theory in mathematics and economics for a solution that meets the objective of both. This may be good sometimes, or too complicated at other times.

If I were to choose one illustration of a typical but famous trial that demonstrates the many bad aspects of the law, its creation, its application, and the difference between civil law and criminal law, it is the trial of Jesus. Here was a man that used speech to educate people about a subject. It should be free speech. It is a civil issue and he should have the right to do it. As typical, when a group or a government feels threatened by speech, they turn the issue into a criminal issue. That is one of the greatest harm to men: turning a civil issue into a criminal issue. Furthermore, his judgment is put to a jury of people that by a voice vote, and with unknown "quality of the vote" is convicted to death. The whole process is not proper based on the many principles I outlined. Think long and hard about this example to understand the issues. And of course, the damage done is great and irreversible. Now go tell his mother Mary and his father: Oh sorry, we made a mistake in killing your son. How can we compensate you for your loss? How many silver coins is his life worth so we can pay you?

Trial of Socrates

The trial of Socrates to me is another example of the lack of freedom of speech and religion and bad courts. It happened in Athens, Greece, in the year 399 BCE in what today is regarded by many as the West's foundational culture city, and the city that is regarded as a land of freedom and wisdom. Yet, this city saw it fit to put one of its most famous teachers, or philosophers on trial for speaking his mind on: 1. Teaching the youth new ideas, which they said corrupts their minds, and 2. On his atheism which supposedly denies Athenian gods.

If these famous, and historic accusations are true, then Socrates was put on trial for what today we can consider as "lack of freedom of speech" and "lack of freedom of religion" in

Athens. The trial apparently led to a death sentence and his death. According to the source Wikipedia in year 2020, June 13, a writing says "the judgement of the court was death for Socrates; most of the jurors voted for the death penalty (*Apology* 38c), yet Plato provides no jury-vote numbers in the text of the *Apology of Socrates*; but Diogenes Laërtius reports that 280 jurors voted for the death penalty and 220 jurors voted for a pecuniary fine for Socrates".

This exemplifies another case of bad laws, and bad method of judging, although having about 500 jurors (sample size) is great and a good consideration to learn from.

Reading Socrates defence argument in court which was supposedly attended by Plato who recorded the defence speech, I was saddened by the arguments made. Socrates said "I did not say this and that ..." etc. instead of making a more fundamental argument such as "what business for you is what I think or say or teach?" If the numbers are true, was sentenced to death by a 280 to 220 vote, which is 56% YES to 46% NO, which is 10% Accuracy Level! And 5.6% Accuracy Of The Yes part of the Vote. What a tragedy in ignorance of mathematics and logic.

Concrete examples of how flawed or immature logic leads to loss of freedom and drives creation of laws and bad solutions:

A Muslim person wants freedom for allowing multiple wives because it is allowed by his religion, but he hates alcohol that is banned by his religion.

While a Christian likes freedom for drinking alcohol maybe because it was Jesus's first miracle of converting water to wine for people to celebrate, but may dislike the multiple wives idea.

The Muslim focuses on what he "dislikes" and tries to pass a law to ban alcohol, which takes away the right and joy of a Christian person. The Christian focuses on what he "dislikes" and tries to pass a law against allowing multiple wives.

If both succeed, the Muslim loses one right, and the Christian loses one right. Other individuals not involved also lose two rights. That is a very bad result of loss for all.

If The Muslim focuses on what he "likes" instead, and lives happily being able to do it, without interfering with others, and if the Christian focused on what he "likes" instead, and lives happily being able to do it, without interfering with others, no one loses, and both are able to practice their "likes" in life. Other individuals are not affected badly by this. This is a winning result for all, with freedom preserved, and no laws created. The Muslims can have their multiple wives if they wish, and the Christians can have their alcohol if they wish, etc. All should be happy, and freedom should prosper because they understand how it works and its benefits.

So a good principle is: Live your life as you wish, and mind your own business, and do not interfere in how others choose to live their life.

To make this rigorous mathematically, a political scientist can develop the formulas to show gains and losses. Not difficult.

One important index to have is "The Ignorance and Threat Index", as I have done in my books, to measure the threat from a person, a group, or a country, based on their level of practice of these principles. If their social intelligence level is low, measured mathematically against the principles in this book, then these individuals, groups or countries can have a "high social threat level" against others. This threat can be minimal when they are weak, and will become apparent and manifest itself when they become strong. So a small minority of Muslims may not be able to implement their agenda as laws, but if they become strong, this tends to automatically change. Same for an Orthodox Jew who may want to force closing business on Saturday, or a Christian group that wants to enforce community standards, or anti-abortion laws, or other special interest groups. All such people would like to limit others, instead of happily enjoying the things they like and have. They are focused on others, instead of themselves. These are threatening individuals, to other's freedom, wellbeing, happiness, and can be a physical threat also when they become strong. They may use the gun, or the law as a gun, to enforce their views.

How Freedom-Of-Choice Can Win

There are groups that advocate "Freedom Of Choice For Self-Defense". This means the right to own and carry a weapon unconcealed anywhere in public. There are other groups who strongly oppose such freedom of choice. If the group that wants to have a law enacted for such Freedom Of Choice For Self-Defense, then it needs public support.

This group may have 20% public support, and 80% opposition. This group alone, advocating more freedom of choice cannot usually win in politics or law making.

There are groups that advocate "Freedom Of Choice For Nudity". This means the right to be nude in public. There are also groups who strongly oppose such freedom of choice. If this group wants to have a law for such freedom of choice then it needs public support.

The group may have 20% of the public in favour and 80% opposed. This group alone, advocating more freedom of choice cannot usually win in politics or law making.

So, the public support for a political candidate that favours Freedom Of Choice For Self-defense law and Freedom Of Choice for Nudity has become 4% of the public. 20% * 20% = 4% support. In probability theory, if half the people wear blue coats and half the people drink beer, the chance of finding a person that wears a blue coat and drinks beer is the chance of finding a blue coat person multiplied by the chance of finding beer drinking person.

Now, if there is a group that wants Freedom Of Choice for Taxation, that is, making taxation voluntary, optional and only imposed on those who like and want taxation, and those who hate force-imposed or involuntary-non-sale or non-service-based taxation may have 20% of the public in favour and 80% opposed.

So the public support for an official candidate that favours Freedom Of Choice For Self-defense law and Freedom Of Choice for Nudity and Freedom Of Choice for Taxation has become 4% * 20%, which is a total of less than 1% support!

Now, if there is a group that wants Freedom Of Choice for Abortion (or building churches), that is, making abortion optional, or non-interference in church affairs, the group may have 20% public and 80% opposition.

So, the public support for an official candidate that favours Freedom Of Choice For Self-defense law and Freedom Of Choice for Nudity and Freedom Of Choice for Taxation and Freedom Of Choice for Abortion has become 0.8% * 20% which is far below 1% support.

I hope you can see the pattern. Those special interest groups will lose, because they want Freedom Of Choice for their own cause, but reject Freedom Of Choice for other's cause! So, the question becomes: Are you for freedom? Freedom Of Choice for you AND others, or are you only for your own Freedom Of Choice? If you want Freedom Of Choice only for you, then you are likely to lose in elections. If you want Freedom Of Choice for everyone, then it is possible to win. Freedom Of Choice means freedom for you to be able to choose, not freedom for you to restrict others from being able to choose. If you support Freedom Of Choice, this means supporting your Freedom Of Choice for Gun Ownership and supporting other's Freedom Of Choice, such as Freedom Of Choice For Nudity, Freedom Of Choice For Abortion, Freedom Of Choice for Taxation. Now, getting together, all of you can win, and none is likely to lose. You will not lose because if you do not like gun ownership, or nudity or abortion etc., then you do not have to practice it. You can live your life as you like, unhindered by others, and others can live their lives as they like, unhindered by you. I will support your Freedom Of Choice to live as you please, and support my Freedom Of Choice so I can live as I please. We can oppress one another or we can free one another. This is "Freedom Coalition" building to remove laws which is the opposite of "Oppression Coalition" that aims to add laws.

Now the mathematics. A candidate that favours all these special groups will have 20% general public support from those favouring gun ownership, and 20% from supporters of nudity, and 20% supporters of optional taxation, and 20% supporters of abortion, and the candidate already has 80% public support (for simplicity, I assume no overlap between groups). If the public understood this simple idea of "are you for freedom of choice for all or just your own freedom of choice?", they can, gather under such a motto, and you and those supporting freedom of choice win. If you make this your public position with other groups, for introducing, selecting, and supporting candidates, then in an extremely brief time, with proper educational campaigns, the world map of politics and freedom may be turned upside down from its current state of evil and ignorance, to a world full of freedom of choice.

Examples of how governments and groups use bad events to rob freedoms: As of the year 2019, maybe around 1 million die from heart disease every years and it is not big news, and one million die from normal flu every year and it is not big news, one million die or injured from normal accidents and it is not big news, etc. and then when sometimes 10 or 100 or 10000 or more die from crime or terror or some health epidemic, then the whole world comes to end and a government declares emergency laws, and calls for suspending civil rights and suspending rational thinking that demands putting numbers and events in perspective. These people find a purpose for their life and to justify their jobs. I maybe sorry for your many deaths and how it happened, but life is full of risks and problems, and that is no excuse to rob my freedom. Do not let those who are against freedom use such incidents to limit freedom and increase their own powers and agendas. There are many known and hidden powers in the world that have their own interests. Be strong-footed in your understanding, and do not let them trespass on our freedoms. You are helping evil when you are weak in your understanding. Risks are a natural part of life, and under no circumstance, does the government has the right to decide this risk for me.

Example of using more freedom, not less, to solve big problems. Scarcity Of Freedom:

As typical in many countries. A group of individuals threaten terror, demonstrations, or blocking people or government businesses, because they feel they have been deprived of some right. The answer is not to take away their freedom of speech or to fight them physically, but better maybe to facilitate that they can be heard by the public to explain their grievance. So they maybe gifted a radio or TV or internet with the inscriptions on it "if you cannot convince the people to support you by talking to them freely, then you want to convince them by force of arm? Is this how we should treat you? We will if you cannot understand this simple logic" so that they can speak as much as they want. This is how problems should be solved, by discussion, they will be told. This with the absolute understanding, that "now you can explain endlessly to the public, but if the public is not convinced, you no longer have the right to take arms, or else, we will take arms against you rightfully as this is your preference for how to resolve issues, and we will kill you mercilessly".

When is it legitimate for citizens to take arms against the government? When any of the civil rights are limited, for any reason, or under any pretext such as emergency situation, war, health epidemics, crimes, terrorism, etc.,

There are many dangers in life to a person, of getting killed, or harmed, etc., but the government should not prevent this citizen from the above freedoms and to take as much risk as he wants in his life. If other citizens feel in danger from his actions, they, not the government, can take the actions they feel are proper to protect their own safety. The freedom of such action resides with the citizen and not the government.

If the above rights are always preserved, then a citizen is not justified to take arms, because his ability to live freely and to communicate his ideas and grievances peacefully are not interfered with in any practical way. If these rights are violated, then he has logical right to take arms against the government. Therefore, by observing and guarding these rights, citizens learn and insist on peaceful resolution to problems.

Translating ideals to reality example: Extremely central to the issue of freedom, and if it can become a reality in practice is the issue of birth control. Scarcity Of Sex: Freedom means freedom for men and freedom for women. If a woman does not have very effective and very accessible means for birth control, her most basic focus would be on birth, because birth of a baby effects her life dramatically. It alters her body dramatically. It alters her physical security dramatically because she is less able to fight aggressions. It alters her financial ability and her ability to provide food for herself and shelter because of her physical changes. It lessens her ability to spend time on education, because when pregnant and after birth, she is less able in all areas to have time and resources for her future, and now the much added new responsibilities of having to meet the needs of a new dependent person. All this, and maybe more, shows the seriousness and effect of birth on a woman and how heavily a woman or an intelligent woman needs to think and worry about. It is extremely dramatic. As a result, sex for a woman is a very life altering decision and possibly for the worse. Therefore, without birth control, extremely effective and extremely accessible, an intelligent woman, may opt to not have sex, because of the results. But if having sex is extremely pleasurable, healthy, and therefore, good to practice, how can a woman enjoy all these benefits without suffering bad consequences. A human wants to enjoy life and freedom to have sex, and this burden of not having birth control or being it extremely accessible, is a major block towards this objective, that forces women to adopt very bad habits of worry and avoid sex. This in turn greatly effect men and their needs to have and enjoy sex to their satisfaction. If men don't have easy access to sex, they will develop bad habits such as masturbation or faggotery, etc. to meet their needs. To justify their new bad habits, they change their psychology for worse to comfort themselves, and adopts possibly one of the psychologies of the uneducated, evil or ugly etc. The results are bad for the person involved and others because he will demand for laws, and for others to change to be like him, to form groups to force others to accept him, and use laws and other mechanisms towards this end. These laws and new social norms etc. are damaging to good values (good health, good hygiene, lots of healthy sex, healthy bodies, healthy psychology, security, freedom, prosperity, etc.) Therefore, if woman do not have easy access to birth control, it causes her extreme damage, to her freedom, and other aspects of life, and the worries she will have, have a dramatic chain effect that alters social norms and habits. Not having birth control effects men for the worse, and it dramatically damages a particular woman's choices and ability to have a good life, or the life she chooses to have. Men's lives are dramatically affected for better or worse by her decision. Limiting her choices and ability limits man's choices and ability, and therefore, it is extremely important for a woman to have this choice and not to live in fear of the consequences of having sex. Men and women should strive not only to protect this right, but to ensure she feels very free to indulge in sex without fear of bad consequences. Those who oppose this, want to control human happiness, and tend to have the psychology of the uneducated, weak, ugly or evil. They are the seeds and power of bad, unliberated, uneducated cultures. This is one example of how to translate ideals such as "freedom, the freedom of choice" from an ideal, such as "the government has no right to interfere in a human (woman's) choice " into making it a reality, by having society and business provide products or solutions to birth control, that also allow meeting good values (healthy and pleasurable sex that is easily accessible). I don't know how to say it better, but few things are as important as this freedom and making it a reality for humans, as it greatly effects their happiness, civility, culture, aggressiveness, and entire healthy development and wellbeing, and costs nothing or little. This subject should be studied well and expanded on.

Shame And Human Freedom

Some of the most basic psychological problems that human suffer and effects their development relate to shame. When shame becomes associated with natural activities that humans do, then it becomes a problem. If a person steals from another person and feels shame, then this is good, but if a person is using a visible to all toilet in an open public space, then there is no shame in the activity. A human being needs to defecate, and it is a natural and essential body function, and interfering in it by creating shame for doing it in public, is creating severe harm to our internal hidden function. Normally, children when born, simply defecate any time they want, to meet internal function needs, such as a full stomach or intestines, etc. This is the proper standard for body function. The body knows its needs best, and interfering with it can be very harmful. It can cause internal invisible function harm. So you can find parents with babies, and when the babies defecate anywhere and anytime, it is a natural act. In recent times and locations, people wanted their children as they mature to use specific location for defecating, and forces the children to learn to hold and control the urge to defecate until they reach the specific location, which some call it a bathroom, or comfort room, etc. The ability to control defecation release takes a long time to develop. And since it starts from earliest age, it is associated with the strongest human functions that humans develop. Therefore, interfering with this function in a bad way, such as making the act of defecating a shame, is labelling and interfering with this normal function that causes no shame. It is like meeting a person eating and looking down upon him, simply because he is eating. Eating is a natural and necessary function, and it would be improper and injurious for others to shame that person for eating. If in these so called "modern times" where people are shamed if they are seen defecating, and the toilets they may use are locked behind private walls, over time, the act of defecating visibly has become an act of shame. A mother or father seeing their children's penis or breast or vagina, without any sexual thought, has similarly become an act of shame. Many very harmful fears also have developed. Man are supposed to worry about seeing the penis of another man, and is supposed to maybe feel threatened by this as a "competitive threat", and a woman is made to feel shame to see another woman breast also as a possible "competitive threat". Is the man's penis too big or too small? Are the woman's breast too big or too small? Such questions which are of little consequences now, have been made so dominant that they have blinded humans from understanding. How big do you want a woman's breast to be? Size 1, 2, 3, 4 or 50? When is big, big enough? And why do you want them so big? Breasts are for food for a baby? Are you a big hungry baby? And can you not get your food from another source? Modern marketing has effected humans psychology greatly, by creating artificial needs. If a product is presented to the market with important people using the product, etc., then a herd impulse among many uneducated to do the same can affect them without much thinking. So if a bra maker shows beautiful women with big breasts using their bras and they label these woman as beautiful, then an association may be made between beautiful and big breasts. If big breasts are desirable, because they provide much milk, then this is understandable. The breast beauty comes from a great needed function packaged in a beautiful design. Function and form are excellent. But to see something as beautiful or not, and as shameful or not without reason, without good logic behind it can be harmful. Now, consider a woman with very big breasts at age 18 years old, and by age thirty or forty, etc., her breasts may sag greatly, a sign of decay of the breast, and become unattractive. Therefore, functionally, when we consider gain and loss analysis for a woman, having big breasts may seem like a bad idea. A woman may want beautiful functional breasts for all or most of her life, not just few years. She may want a beautiful body for all or most her life, not just a few years. And, very big breasts can cause strain on the back, causing deformation in the body. Big breasts would seem to be a negative factor for a human that wants a healthy body that is capable of running, agility, flexibility, doing sports or other physical function. Looking at these factors, when can see that in our times, the years around 2020, we see many woman are made to feel shame if they have a natural and very healthy and functional smaller breasts, that stay youthful till their old age. Many such woman are made embarrassed by their beautiful breasts, because of marketing or ignorant culture, that taught them since early age, that smaller breasts means a woman, is not a developed woman. But the analysis shows the opposite, and breasts that are proportional to the size of the woman, and for needed body functions of posture, mobility, agility, etc. are better. Women have developed shame of their body, when there is no shame, and should not be. Today, being nude is practically illegal all over the world. It is not only a social taboo, it is banned by law. This allows woman who already feel shame about their breasts, to be comforted by wearing clothes. Two bad ideas: shame and the law, feeding on each other to destroy human psychology. Instead of women showing their breasts in public any time they want to, and the same for their vagina, they are unable to do it. What sounds good to today's many uneducated humans, is very harmful to humans. Same for men. Many men today are made to feel shame about showing or seeing a penis in public. As with woman's breasts analysis, the focus on function and form of the penis has been lost. If big breasts falsely meant femininity, out of desire to feed the hunger of a child, and was made a symbol of fertility over time, a big penis to many today, is being made to be associated with manhood or being a man. Use your own analysis to understand. Should a mouse-size female mate with an elephant-size male? Should a mouse-size male mate with an elephant-size female? Compatibility in size can be a very important factor. And should humans be the size of elephants? Is being elephant size compatible with the ideal form and body function of a human? There is no need for me to go into every detail in my limited health ability to write. But almost complete change in attitudes is needed. When evangelizers from different religions walked or broke into peaceful ancient human settlements that lived in their own ways for thousands or much more, natural, nude, not knowing shame for this. One of the first acts these strangers, so-called civilized-people did, was to make or encourage these "uncivilized savages" to dress, and created shame in them for being nude, which corrupted a most important human attribute, which is "to not be ashamed of their own body and being nude." Few are the damages that have been done to mankind as this.

I already explained that no law should exist in any such matters or others. To help remember these facts, and to be able to fight back the onslaught of marketing and the many uneducated people trying to control the lives of others, it is important to develop smart habits and actions. Therefore, when you make a place for defecating, let it always be visible, such as having transparent glass walls. Defecating is a natural act. Some may prefer to not smell what happens during the act, and ventilation can solve such problems. Try to make your surroundings beautiful. Make your toilet place as other places, surrounded by the things you love, flowing water falls, trees, plants and flowers, etc. Create beauty around you, and have nothing to be ashamed of, neither in body, nor natural functions. If you are unsatisfied with your body for good reason, try to find a solution. Do not let others shame you for no good reason, and one way you can fight this human bad tendency is by nudity and transparency. You will become smarter and stronger. Otherwise, any such shame allowed can be used by some as the seed of a tree to grow and make you lose.

One idea came to me while I tried to find solutions to such problems was to request from the Pope to be nude in public. This single act by such a person would in a single day transform attitudes worldwide, and would cause the people to demand end of many laws, which would solve many human psychological problems and create much more freedom, that may quickly turn into complete freedom. Clothe can protect and be used for protection from the uneducated by the clergy, but when cloth become permanent, for security, then the uneducated and enemies of man have already won. I hope the Pope will act on this, especially when he looks up the ceilings of the Vatican. The Jain people, mostly of India, are extremely small in number and their culture and traditions have been destroyed or restricted and freedom taken away. Their top monk is nude in the temple, and their freedom to be nude anywhere has been severely restricted, as the freedom of most humans have. It is good to know who is for human freedom and who is not.

One amusing thought about shame. As a young boy in Lebanon I started to mature around the age of 13, in a so-called "conservative culture" that looked down on man-woman interaction and limited freedom of interaction severely. I started to experience the urge to have sex, but having the problem of not being allowed to freely interact with women socially and especially sexually. There was no choice but to masturbate to release this imposed urge and impulse. Instead of being with a young girl, in a relaxed environment just enjoying ourselves in freedom and no fear, I would lock myself in a private room and masturbate. A very bad solution, and much later in my life and after marriage and having children, I started to call such cultures "Faggot Cultures" because they forced men and women into unnatural acts, deviant acts, to meet their natural physical needs. I greatly disliked what their ignorant values did to human beings and their development, and as of today, this includes most cultures on earth. But the Lebanese have a very long history, that far long ago, different from today, seemed to have been endowed with much intelligence. Some of this intelligence remains as a heritage. So when the maturing teens in my town wanted to start masturbating, they would joke saying: "Start singing the national anthem". We wanted to masturbate to the tune of the national anthem, and we joked about it. So much deep wisdom was in this, it is hard to describe. The national anthem, usually a sacred symbol to many, along with culture, tends to take the freedom of people, instead of giving it, by creating improper mindless emotionalism, that can create social restriction or legal restrictions, that force humans into such acts, which cause men and women to masturbate instead of making love to each other. Also, the idea of nationalism seemed like such a strange idea to humans of the past who interacted and roamed the earth freely when they could, without much interference. But the worst idea that kept coming to mind was "Are women trying to make men faggots by supporting such poor cultures and laws that prevent freedom of sexuality?" When I analysed this, I could understand a woman saying "You want to ruin my future and life just for one sex act? Do you understand the consequences for me? How my life path changes from having one child?" And I tried to explain to all in my writings how important it is for women to have complete control over having a baby or not, because if she cannot protect herself from pregnancy, she may wisely hold back on having sex, and this have gigantic bad consequences for the kind of culture that develops from her choice.

Nudity, clothing, transparency and freedom of choice

It is extremely important to facilitate the basic ingredients that make freedom easy to practice. One such item is clothing. Clothing can be a necessity due to weather, protection from injury or for hygiene. If some want to practice nudity at all time, and equally important to maintain full transparency in their life, by having their body visible in full, then it is important to create excellent wearable fabrics and material that are transparent. Fabrics that meet the needs in softness, durability, and other desirable properties so that they can easily compete with common material. When such transparent materials are available, people can wear clothing in all weather and conditions and maintain the great and needed benefits of visible nudity and full personal transparency.

Towards this end, I wanted to start such a company, but my condition does not allow me now, so I hope many other designers and basic material manufacturers will, speedily, as one of the most important visible factors that promote healthy behavior and preserves freedom of choice. Clothing has become a central component in the disappearance of freedom, where humans in past history were seemingly constantly nude, and by necessity, or religions were made to wear clothes. As this happened, the focus of beauty can shift from seeing the beauty of a nude body and judging it properly, to seeing a clothed body, and judging the clothes, especially as unattractive bodies find cover and comfort in clothes, that helps in distraction from their reality. This comfort can become so great for them to the point of them wanting it to be the standard practice on all people, in creating taboos in a culture, or by use of law. Practicing this bad behavior, after a short time, can make clothing an issue that is very powerful, with most people not being of attractive body standards, give great support and legitimacy to preventing nudity, under different real or contrived reasons. Instead of taking pride in their bodies being well maintained, a partial sign of intelligence, they take pride and comfort in clothes. Their are other factors that drives the trend for clothing, such as businesses that develop around this industry that make clothing's importance self-sustaining. Whole cultures, religions, and politics can grow from such simple beginnings to develop far and leave their origins invisible. Mandate clothing is one of the most important hidden enemies of personal freedom of choice, and so central in human psychology, it is central in some mythology and religious stories, that nude Adam, in the story in Genesis of the Bible, was comfortable in his nudity, until he was made to feel shame in nudity, not from nudity being wrong, but from knowing too much about the ways of gods or spirits, when he ate from the forbidden tree of knowledge. I had spoken about how men have become ashamed to be nude or see other men nude, and same for women, and same for seeing each other nude. Few things have harmed mankind as this improper perception and behavior.

It is important to understand the difference between nude people that are nude by necessity of poverty or lack of education, and rich or educated people nude because of their intelligence. The first will abandon nudity for a donated piece of clothe to appear rich, while the second will not because they understand and love freedom of choice and the enormous benefits of transparency.

Similarly, poor or uneducated people with freedom, randomly developed in their culture, a culture made out of poverty of culture and economy, are unaware of freedom as a concept, are different people from rich or educated people who insist on complete freedom in their culture, that is the absence of law, because they are completely aware that "we insist on freedom, no laws, as we insist that man not rule over another by force of gun, or force of law." Two cultures living in freedom, the first may abandon it for a donated piece of clothe or a meal, while the second will likely fight, and may fight heaven and earth to not allow freedom's absence.

It is easy to adopt nudity when children practice it, transparency (honesty and openness) and good thinking from early life. Towards this end, I hope schools will use this book for part of their studies, and I grant them use at free cost. I hope advanced "learning in freedom of exploring" schools will adopt this book.

The difference between beauty and temptation is important to understand

If a person wants to be "free", "peaceful", and "intelligent", it is important to practice your ideas if they are correct. To not do so, therefore, is incorrect behaviour.

If a beautiful woman or man waked by, an object of beauty that you see as beautiful. If that beautiful person is aware of their beauty, there are several situations to consider. Here are some:

1. This beautiful person uses this awareness to intentionally excite others sexually, to gain an advantage. It is their right to do so.

2. This beautiful person uses this awareness to intentionally excite others sexually, to gain an advantage, and "forcefully" makes you turn your head by sending a person to do so, by grabbing you by the neck or head, to turn it and see. It is NOT their right to do so.

3. If humans are to be free, they should be able to walk nude anywhere they wish in public, without attacking others, or being attacked by others.

It is important to understand the nuances of nudity and temptation, and the skills of temptation, to be aware how mankind has deviated from freedom. Freedom is important to me, and I want you to understand that the most basic demonstration of your awareness of freedom and its benefits, is to be nude in public.

When I remember my dad, the Digambar Jains who have been savaged, and Guillermo Tolentino, and the ceilings of the Vatican, I remember beautiful things. And I like it when beauty and truth are the same.

Freedom is less meaningful with scarcity, example:

Very important: Must add. On prostitution. It seems that a woman that has sex with a man or masturbate him should not charge money if she gets pleasure out of it. And if as a general principle it is wise to enjoy your work, it seems wise that the sex worker should enjoy it. And if she enjoys it a lot, then maybe she should not charge for it. As for me, a man, I have no problem doing this work if safe. While I will hesitate to give a woman sex for fear of disease, I do not hesitate from masturbating her for free. By playing with her breast and maybe other parts of her body. I am willing to do it for free if I find the woman attractive. No need to feel any shame about such work. It can be very pleasurable when safe, and it can be very healing or stress reducing to the customer. Do not shame these workers, rather appreciate the wonderful service they offer. It can be the most healing service or therapy you can have. This is a mere service and is not the same as selling your body.

And one sign to know if a culture is bad, is finding out how much they limit or discourage natural healthy sex. A bad culture creates artificial scarcity in sex. This scarcity has many supporters, and is then used by some woman to force men into marriage (in part to satisfy their sexual needs) or make it a financial trade for women. Others will use it for anti-freedom social agendas. I will repeat again how important it is for learning about safe sex and practicing it often as a very healthy and pleasurable activity and to avoid making it a scarcity. Meantime, create lots of high quality sex toys for men to satisfy their sexual urges and lessen being controlled by these urges and by women who use this scarcity to control them. Women already seem to have plenty of such toys.

Scarcity of products, such as drugs: Here is something for you to think about, instead of me, to see if you are beginning to understand how to use freedom and abundance to solve problems:

In many countries, the use of so-called drugs is illegal. Punishable by severe punishment. A kilogram of illegal drugs is extremely expensive, and is surrounded by illegal or criminal activities that make prices very high and attractive to engage in. If the government decided to provide or allow these drugs to be sold freely, and easily, will the price per kilogram drop from 50,000 dollars maybe to 5 dollars, just like buying any product in the supermarket? Will all the crime surrounding this economic product stop? Will the users, few hopefully, become a public health issue rather than a criminal issue, to try to help, like any addict or sick individual? Can you understand the economics of scarcity? And how it effects price, crime, and other issues? Can you think of good solutions that respect freedom?

Economic needs and corruption of freedom values. An example: A note about oil fuel and how it corrupts international human values, and international politics for the worse. Countries with maybe decent values become political slaves and opponents of freedom for fear of badly needed product shortage. They corrupt their values, and instead of like-minded countries being aware of being made into an economic hostage, and acting in solidarity, doing a reverse and complete boycott of such hostile countries. Whatever the answer is, it should be a clear unmistakable and effective and collective peaceful reply. Few commodities have corrupted international values as oil. It should be studied well as to how deal with such issues.

History Shows Success Of Coerciveness and Oppression

Recent history of the last few hundred years is well documented, and shows that coerciveness or oppression were the government model almost universally adopted. The question of why has this happened must be answered clearly if people are not to keep repeating this error, given a choice of freedom, unless people choose oppression as a better model for human relations.

Examining oppression and its success, I concluded that ignorance was a primary reason. If people were presented with other options and understood them well, then oppression would not have spread as the proper government model. Being ignorant of other government models, oppression brought many of the people benefits. An important benefit came from oppression because it can be a very effective tool or mechanism for "capital formation" and "labor formation". The fact that the system is oppressive can be of little consequences to some, if they see suitable short-term-results being produced for them, than what their previous free society did. So if these generally-uneducated people choose to elect a thief and tyrant to lead, or he made himself, a ruler, then this tyrant thief, may confiscate peoples' daily wages, and give them back a portion of it, and he keeps a portion, to dedicate for every worker or person, as saving for his future old age or when in severe need. Typically, an intelligent person does this for himself without being forced into it, so he may feel it is an act of aggression and interference by strangers in his personal affairs and property. While an unintelligent person, if rich and his money is confiscated by others to force him to save for the future, will see this as good behavior from strangers, because they are ensuring his future, and will not become a burden on others, or sees strangers as he sees his parents, a caretaker of his future. If he was intelligent, he would do what is intelligent, without being forced by others to do it. So if you know the principle "do not steal from others or damage their property", and you are intelligent enough to know this is a good principle to live by, then you do it by yourself, and you would not want strangers forcing this on you, by creating a tyrannical system that puts two guards around you 24 hours a day, monitoring your every action, just to ensure you do not steal. And what if someone stole your property and you went to his house and stole it back? Is this stealing by you? Do you need a court system to decide if you or he is the thief? and will the judge know the true facts and rule correctly? You can see it can get extremely complicated and in a tyrannical system, it seems you must have complete tyranny for the system to work, or you can have a freedom-of-choice system and those involved, are alone involved, and it is for them to resolve all issues, without interference from strangers. Another issue is if the person is unintelligent AND poor. This is a bad combination, because if such a person sees good progress in his personal life, he is not likely to understand that his progress is coming at the expense of innocent people whose properties or freedom-of-choice are being forcefully taken. If he had no food or a job, and now he does, he is likely to look only one level deep, and be thankful to this tyrant thief for the benefits, as the beneficiaries of Robin Hood's theft were. The person does not look deeper , one more level, or is incapable of looking deeper, to see that the job or food he received is the result of food or money being forcefully taken (stolen) from another person.

Therefore, we can see how a tyrant ruler thief can quickly generate capital pools, and labor pools, and use them for any purpose. There is an economic reality that has nothing to do with politics or society. When capital is formed in a larger size, more can be done, and if it is on a very large scale, very big things can be done. This is important to understand. Second is the formation of labor. Same applies. Combining the two leads to even greater capabilities. Now you should be able to understand why oppressive governments can easily succeed, get a good reputation, and dominate, even though they are founded on theft. There seems to be a lot of poor people, or uneducated, and these two groups are another foundation of oppression. So how can freedom-of-choice and its few advocates win at our times? It seems to be a near impossible task. But with this book, and others like it, it is possible. And with the mathematics I developed to show the correctness of freedom as a choice, it should be a sure bet that freedom can win, and very quickly. You can argue philosophy a lot, but mathematics can put an end to nonsense because it makes this issue a pure science.

Without providing understandable-free-effective alternatives by those wanting freedom, freedom of choice, oppressive-coercive-systems will likely win. Understanding this issue well is one of the central understandings of why freedom lost until now. I have explained other reasons for such a loss in different books or sections. Now it is time to bring in your best mathematics, simulations, and clear-simple-understandable public education, and the future should look brighter and different.

The Three Needed Factors For Freedom In Hostile Environments

Therefore, for freedom-of-choice systems to win against oppressive-coercive systems, the people need: - Ingrained cultural knowledge of the critical importance of "capital formation" and the practice of how to build it.

- Extremely important is ingrained cultural knowledge of labor formation and how to build it.

- last needed component is ingrained cultural knowledge of the principle "we do not allow man to rule over man, by force of gun or force of law".

With these three components in place, no longer would a person looking at a newborn gazelle, seconds after birth, see it far outrun a newborn human, and conclude the gazelle is a superior being to a human. The human baby may take a year or two just to walk, and more time to run and develop, but few years later, the human may be a million times more capable Than the gazelle.

Now, as humans concerned for our own welfare, which by necessity forces us to consider how other humans' ignorance effect us, can feel more secure that a person looking at coercive systems or coercive relations understands what is going on, and that he or she will be on the side of freedom-of-choice systems. Poverty in most of its dimensions comes from cultural poverty. And at the roots of a good culture are well established scientific principles.

Understanding External Oppression Versus Internal Oppression

There are many great national heroes in countries that acquired their status because they fought external aggression, such as an occupying power or were involved in a war of self defense, but did nothing or understood little about internal aggression. I do not consider such acts by such heroes as sufficient, without their understanding and opposition to internal aggression as well. Examples from history:

 - USA Patriots fought to death the British for imposing a "Tea Tax" on them , but never fought to death their own government doing maybe 1000 times more aggression by imposed taxation and loss of freedom of choice.

 - The British people split from the European Union to regain control of their money system, yet, those same British people never took the next logical step, to split from their own government or dispose of it completely.

 - The Russians fought the German Invasion, yet went ahead itself to occupy by force many foreign lands. And they had fought German control of them, yet failed to fight a much worse internal system that controlled them.

 - The examples go on and on, for almost every country, where they make distinction between external aggression and internal aggression, when they should not, as if being raped by a foreign person is worse or different from being raped by a fellow country person you don't know, or a friend or relative you know.

A very brief note about forms of government

A central government by its nature, its dynamics, its mathematical model, combined with citizenry uneducated in logic tend to be biased to concentrate power and control at the expense of freedom of choice. Its opposite form of government is decentralized governance, where control is pushed away from the center, all the way to the edge of the system, which is the individual. This I think is a far superior system, that preserves complete freedom of choice, which should be a primary focus of an educated person. However, this system in general requires citizens who are highly educated in this subject, to understand how such a system works, its benefits, and how it compares with a centralized system. I have explained in this book and others how the uneducated, the poor, the disadvantaged can be easily manipulated or have internal incentives to create or seek solutions from a central government and are mindless about taking away others' freedom. These driving forces to create a central government can be extremely strong, and once in motion, have great momentum to continue, and get stronger. How to educate to guard against these ills in thinking and behaviour is a difficult task, but it is a task that some of us should undertake, if they are capable of doing it. The cost of not doing it is very high to individuals like me, who want to live in a good system.

Learning how to create and manage capital formation and resource formation in a poor environment is an antidote to central government driving forces, and is very important to allow freedom to flourish on strong foundations. If the people are uneducated they are likely to be poor also. Lack of education and poverty makes an individual vulnerable in many ways, but concerning freedom, it makes them easy to sway in other directions, where they will support government laws and programs that give them, without care or realization of the consequences. They want schools, roads, electric networks being built, and they fall in love with government and its ability. They were never taught how to collect their resources to build the needed schools, roads, and other projects. Here are some examples of the top of my head:

Example 1: A teacher in a small town, calls on other teachers to get together to form a needed school. Maybe students sit under a tree, under a tent, or inexpensive room built by locals who volunteer this, or are paid later. The problem is solved locally, and youngsters get an education.

Example 2: A person in the village creates gambling games for locals. They play dice games and card games that cost almost nothing to create. They have daily or weekly lottery. This is a great **capital formation** business. The lottery winner can take the wins, to start a small business, and may not gamble again, and if he does, he knows he is participant in capital formation for others and not in gambling. The winner is given by the owner a single sheet of paper saying "you can start your business in one day, and here are the basic steps, the rest is intelligence, with time, and effort added"

Example 3: A person with very little money, alone, or with other friends or families, decide to start a micro loans business.

Example 4: A woman used a very small loan to buy two chickens. Every day, the chicken gave eggs. In one week, the chicken gave 14 eggs, that a month later became 14 chicks. She was on her way to have a good living from the eggs sold, and the chicken farm she developed. In rural areas, chicken roam and do not need feed.

Example 5: A poor family used a lottery win to buy 5 small goats for milk. Goats roam to eat. The family was on its way to have needed income. In rural areas, all you need for daily living are few pesos, or the food to consume. Milk and its by-products are needed food for some.

Example 6: In a town, a person asked an engineer, a manager, a loan business man, an accountant, if they would join him to form a company or cooperative, to start a needed small electric company. He offered every one of these people an equal share in the company. No one was paid till revenues started. And every time they needed a specialist or employee to add, they offered them a percentage ownership in the company, by each existing owner giving a share of his share. This way, they can have all the needed experts and employees without having money to pay them. Future gains were enough to entice them. Others were motivated to see the project done. They taught this method of **resource formation** to all adults in town. They can now start creating needed companies, big and small with no capital, just smart pooling of people, friends and family members.

Side Note: If economic output is the product of intelligence, labor and capital, what is the order of their in importance, assuming you can define these factors mathematically. And which one, when it changes (mathematical derivative) , produces the greatest return on investment in it? Intelligence or labor or capital? What is the set of equations that define an optimum solution? Is intelligence the most important part? Can you fit freedom into the intelligence part?

Example 7: Having learned capital and resource formation, a small very poor town without school, good food, or electricity, was able to have a school, egg shop, milk shop, meat shop, and electricity. They developed the good value of asking "how do we solve this problem ourselves?" And using simple easy to understand tools in their bag, tools for capital formation, and resource formation, they felt more confident in being able to solve their own problems and became immunized from the bad logic of other humans that call for a central government that in turn by force of law steal other people's money and freedom.

Example 8: A person looked at his fellow town people and thought they should have more opportunity to interact together, for many benefits, especially to increase his joy and theirs. So he gathered a group of his friends that can play music instruments and sing, to form a daily fiesta in the evening that did not cost a single peso to create. It is typical to have a fiesta festival only once a year, but these people were singing and dancing daily in the town center, changing the town and its people's daily happiness level dramatically.

Example 9: A health conscious person seeing how the fiesta festival was created and its success, decided to create a similar daily health event, where people came to play fun sports games as their method for daily exercise. Men and women and children who looked physically unfit and unattractive, started to improve their health dramatically while having fun.

If the project is small or big, or gigantic, and if the town is small, big, or as big as a country, such principles for solving problems in a private nongovernmental way can be used.

Wikipedia online internet free encyclopaedia of recent years, is one of many examples of what one person can do, with his knowledge and the smart aggregation of the power of many people on a single massive project. Such efforts can inspire many, and in different domains.

When people understand how freedom works, and see its benefits, they will become effective supporters for it.

Mathematically, because officials need to be elected with 99%+ votes to be high quality or elected with high accuracy. The same is for creating laws. Same for court verdicts. Achieving these results seems impossible looking at actual practice results. Therefore, the idea of a central government is not practically implementable if it is to have 99%+ qualities.

The freedom to own and carry a gun is the most important freedom there is. You have the right to protect yourself, without reliance on anyone.

One country seems to escape human stupidity in regard to gun control. Switzerland, where not only guns, but machine guns can be bought easily, supposedly. Switzerland must have some of the smartest people on earth. They have these things known about them:

They are supposed to have the best wrist watches in the world. Which indicates a good knowledge of science and technological ability.

Even though surrounded by highly rich and advanced European countries technologically, they did not join them (the EU countries) in order not to lose their freedom and independence, and intelligence, maybe. While the EU countries are full of regulations, and buying a gun and carrying it may be prohibited or controlled strictly, the Swiss people attitude on this is different. Few hundred years back, almost in every place on earth, people walked with guns, swords, and no one paid any attention. It was the normal thing to do. If you did not have your gun or sword by your side, that may have seemed very strange.

Supposedly, Switzerland had the best banking system in the world. So they must know about money and economics. A resident or not in few minutes could open a bank account in the most advanced banking system with few questions asked. Now, the rest of the dumb world, interested in control, by coercion I think, with security as a main driving excuse, has tried successfully to interfere in their free system. These dumb governments always have their excellent excuses for interfering and limiting freedom and independence.

They are also known for excellence in many products areas, such as shoes.

Their flag is a big white cross, and the Vatican, which is located in Italy, has none other than the Swiss protect the catholic pope, arguably the most important person on earth, or one of them.

So what does control and regulation bring? The Swiss have shown that regulations are not needed. While free people and markets can create excellence in every area. May they keep the good fight for independence and freedom from regulation, and free gun ownership and carrying, and may they prosper for it.

The examples of the death of freedom of choice seem everywhere, that when I come on a light, that is not even fully bright, it is worth noting.

The voting system of the World Trade Organization

The voting system of the World Trade Organization is a bit unusual in that it requires unanimous vote results. It is an opposite voting system to simple majority voting. I have shown that the simple majority system is flawed, and when fixed, it resembles a unanimous voting system. Interesting that such a voting system exists for major international organization. It looks like a typical case of psychological dissonance, between what people say is important and practice in congress, versus what they accept when they feel their jobs or money is on the line.

Formula for quality of the vote when the number of voters is very large, more than 10,000 maybe, such as in congressional or presidential elections. It is extremely simple to teach the general public:

Accuracy Of The Vote = (%YES - %NO)

A more precise formula is:

Accuracy Of The Vote (accounting for group size) = (%YES -

$$\%NO) - 2 * \frac{0.5}{\sqrt{n}} = (\%YES - \%NO) - \frac{1}{\sqrt{n}}$$

, n is the group size. And this is using the Standard Error formula

An even more precise formula, using the Margin Of Error formula is:

Accuracy Of The Vote (accounting for group size and

confidence of 99.99% in results) = (%YES - %NO) $- \dfrac{4}{\sqrt{n}}$

Even better and a more complete equation, assuming Normal Distributions is:

$$Poll\ Accuracy = (\%YES - \%NO) - \frac{2Z}{\sqrt{n}} * \left(\sqrt{(YES\% * NO\%) + \left(\frac{1}{N} * \left(1 - \frac{1}{N} \right) \right)} \right)$$

The equation is the distance of a poll results distribution (YES~ - NO~)~ from the poll's expected random distribution, multiplied by 2.

Written in a beautiful human language and in simplified form:

$$\lambda = \checkmark - \boxtimes - 4/\sqrt{n}$$

YES% is percent of yes voters $= \checkmark, in\ green = success\ or\ correct$

NO% = 1 - YES% $= \boxtimes\ not\ checkmark, in\ red = not\ success\ or\ not\ correct$

$\lambda = accuracy\ in\ blue,\ Greek\ lower\ case\ lambda\ letter\ or\ chinese\ letter = human = net\ success\ or\ net\ correct$

n is voters group size

$\sqrt{n}\ is\ square\ root,\ or\ square\ side,\ of\ n.$

$If\ n = 100\ voters,\ square\ side\ is\ 10,\ because\ 10x10 = 100.$

$If\ n = 9\ voters,\ square\ side\ is\ 3,\ because\ 3x3 = 9.$

N, N = 2 for {yes , no} answer choices. Note: YES = yes% and NO is NOT YES = 1 - YES in all these options.

Further refinement for accuracy can be accomplished by using different N options for an answer:

N = 3 for { yes , don't know, no} answer choices. For humans, in logic, and in natural language, these 3 points on the logic interval [0 , 1] seem to be the minimum certainty choices that should be offered as choices to an answer.

N = 5 {yes, maybe yes, don't know, maybe no, no} answer choices, in logic, and in natural language seem to be the maximum certainty choice points that should be offered as choices to an answer.

With N = 5 certainty points, you can learn in my other book, form an additional 4 uncertainty regions that are between these certainty points. Using this, we can create three certainty points and four regions, or five certainty points and 4 regions: N=7 {yes, likely yes, maybe yes, don't know, maybe no, likely no, no} or N=9 {yes, likely yes, ?? choose word, maybe yes, don't know, maybe no, ?? choose word, likely no, no} . This seems to be the natural limit of spoken language granulite to answer a question, which is a subject requiring full study by looking at a continuous logic interval [0 , 1].

etc.

(Ignore the following note if too technical: With this, 1/N becomes what technically can be called the expected random mean of a question in a poll, or its random population or random sample mean, from which we can calculate the deviation or standard deviation as in the full accuracy equation above).

Z, is the Statistical Z-Score. Z = 1 gives 68% Confidence Level in computed results.

Z = 2 gives 95% Confidence Level in computed results.

Z = 3 gives 99% Confidence Level in computed results.

Z = 4 gives 99.99% Confidence Level in computed results.

For the first time in recorded human history, humans have a formula to measure group decisions, such as a vote or a poll. With this equation, humans can begin to leave the dark ages behind, and move into the light by "upholding mathematical accuracy, in decision making, as a human heritage".

Which Way Do I Go?

Left or Right?

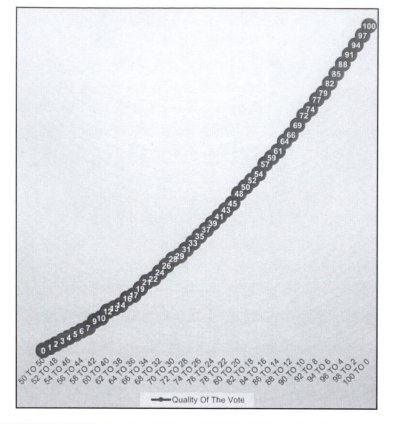

Quality Of The Vote

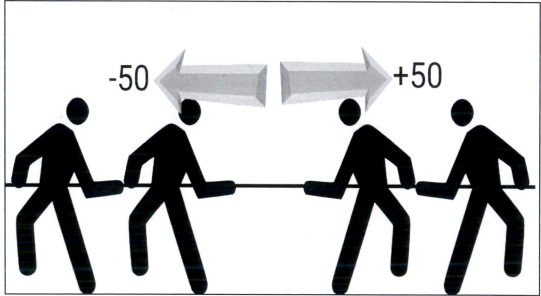

A 50% to 50% vote result has nearly the same guidance confidence level as a 51% to 49% vote result, which is zero. And zero information value.

Objects with zero value belong to the trash can.

The quality of the water, food, decisions, and votes we use should be of good quality.

Now you know why you should not interfere in our life, it is our responsibility and our risks, so here is the Golden Rule Of Freedom:

Mind and Control Your Own Business and Life, Not Mine.

For A Book To Teach Children Important Math Concepts

Here is what may serve as guideline to help you do a children book:

Step 1. Make the subject understandable to the general, non math educated adult population, using common language and common examples that they can relate to in their life.

Step 2. Change the language and examples used one more time, to be understood by children, and using examples children can relate to.

Step 3. Transform these explanations and examples into games children can play.

Step 4. Create physical games that represent these concepts, so that children can play these games. These physical games are best when they are good physical exercises at the same time, if possible to design.

When children physically play these games, they are more likely to understand them, intuitively, and analytically, and to remember them for the long term, and intuitively act on them as problem are encountered, o solutions are needed.

I do not have time or resources to do it. Permission is granted to translate this book to children specific language, and to children games, for these to become a normal part of their physical education exercises.

The Upper Bound Limit Of Court Accuracy

by

Jamil Kazoun

Email: JamilKazoun@Gmail.com

Abstract:

The mathematical statistical theory "Central Limit Theory", and its component the "Standard Error Of The Mean" equation give the amount of error for a specific sample or group size. In a case, if the sample size is equal to one person or one judge, and the probability of the judge being correct is equal to the judge being incorrect, this implies this probability is 0.5. This probability produces a Standard Error of 0.5. This implies the accuracy of a decision by any single judge is limited to 0%.

The Formula for Standard Error (S.E.) is

$$S.E. = sqrt (p * (1 - p)/n)$$

where p is the probability of being correct

and n is the sample size

Since any individual, even a supreme court judge, on any contested issue, as demonstrated by practice where such judges can be in complete and equal opposition to each other, such as a supreme court composed of 10 judges, make a decision with 5 judges voting In Favour and 5 judges voting Oppose, this implies that these well educated and experienced judges have equal chance of being on either side of an argument. They are accorded equal probability of being correct. This means the probability of being In Favor, p, is equal to the probability of being Opposed, q. This implies this probability of a judge being correct is 50% or 0.5, because the probability of the two sides must add up to 1.

$p + q = 1$, and $p = q$

$2p = 1$,

$p = 1/2 = 0.5 = 50\%$

Therefore the S.E. = sqrt (p * (1 - p)/n) =

sqrt (0.5 * (1 - 0.5)/1) = 0.5

S.E. = 0.5

Therefore the Standard Error Of The Mean produced from a single judge decision is 0.5 or 50

The implications for a judicial system that allows a single judge to rule on a contested issue are devastating. Such a system has built in Error rate of 50, which seems absolutely unacceptable. In ancient Athens, the number of judges or jury in a case seems to have been around 500, as cited by some, as in the famous court trial case of Socrates. A sample size of 500 jurors in that case produces a maximum accuracy-reliability for a decision of about 97.7% accuracy. Compare this to 50% accuracy of a single judge decision, or 84% accuracy of a 9 judges jury system, such as the USA Supreme Court.

Conclusion: If there is to be a judge in a court case, we have to determine the amount of acceptable error allowed in a court, and based on that, calculate what the needed number of judges or jury will be. The current system allows a dangerous level of error that is epidemic. This means the current judicial system is fundamentally flawed and requires an immediate halt to all judicial cases, pending a review and a resolution to this problem.

Current Public Voting Systems With Multi Candidates Options Are Flawed

by

Jamil Kazoun

Abstract:

A proof is presented that a multi-way selection voting system is fundamentally flawed because it can produce the wrong result for the desired choice.

Analysis:

If we have more than two candidates in an election, for example, if the choices in a vote were three candidates, Candidate A, Candidate B, and Candidate C, with these facts:

Candidate A has 40% public support with 60% absolutely opposed to him.

Definition: Absolutely Opposed means a voter finds this candidate absolutely unacceptable and would not vote in his favour under any circumstance.

In political terms, the term "Negatives" is used, as in "this person has high Negatives, or his Negatives are 60%".

Definition: Negatives means Absolutely Opposed

Candidate B has 30% support and 20% Absolutely Opposed

Candidate C has 25% support and 20% Absolutely Opposed

Candidate Name	In Favor	Absolutely Opposed	Political View
A	40%	60%	Wants dictatorship
B	30%	20%	Wants freedom of choice
C	29%	20%	Wants freedom of choice

Under many if not all public election systems, Candidate A wins the vote result by having the most In Favour portion of 40%.

Removing from calculation all the personal candidate factors as being equal, such as trust, likability, etc. , then the only remaining factor for a voter to consider is their political views. (Similar to a vote with three choices of a subject and not candidates, as when there is a ballot

question to vote on: "Do you wish: A. No school B. A school built C. A big school built?" These three vote choices, if they have the exact In Favour and Absolutely Opposed numbers as the political candidates example, have no factors such as trust or likability, and are evaluated purely based on the vote choice content.) therefore, it is proper to not let other factors be considered in this analysis.

If it turns out that Candidate B and Candidate C hold nearly identical political views, but are from different political parties, and they together have public support of 59% for their views, then their political views should win, because the public wants candidates B and C views more than other views. But having two candidates with near identical views has split the public support for this view in two, that is the 59% public choice for "freedom" has been divided between the two candidates. If either candidate B or C withdraws from the election, the remaining candidate wins with 59% support. But neither candidate B or C withdraws from the election, and candidate A wins with 40% support for "oppression", which does not represent the public choice of 59% support for "freedom", represented in either of the other two candidates.

But, in a two-way voting selection process, similar to sports teams selection process, the public chooses by a vote in a first round between candidates A and B, or A and C, or B and C. In the next round, the winner is against the remaining candidate. Here are the scenarios:

1. A against B : B wins, then B against C : B wins
2. A against C : C wins, then C against B : B wins
3. B against C : B wins, then B against A : B wins

When candidate C is not in the vote choice, his supporters shift to candidate B. When candidate B is not in the vote choice, his supporters shift to candidate C.

- We can see from this result that candidate B always wins. This is different result than the first voting system which lets candidate A be the winner. Candidate A and candidate B hold opposing views, and this analysis proves that a multi-way voting system produces wrong results, results which do not properly represent the public choice, whether the choices are candidates, or a particular subject.
- The first voting system allows a candidate opposed by a majority of the public to win. Candidate A has 60% public opposition, yet he won. And he won by only 40% support.
- The first voting system has no minimal cutoff or threshold protection point, and allows a candidate to win by nearly any amount of support, even if lower than 50%, or much lower than 50% if the number of candidates and their support and opposition allows. For example, if 10 candidates are in the race, a candidate can win if he only has 10% support, and 90% public opposition, which is the exact opposite of the public choice (9 candidates each getting 9% support and the rest abstaining).

This knowledge incidentally can be used to intentionally skew election results. For example, if initially there are only two candidates in a political election, Candidate A and Candidate B, and candidate A will lose to candidate B, then sinisterly, candidate A can introduce or help a candidate C to enter the election, and this can make him win if the numbers are similar to the example above.

A very important requirement seems to be the need for a proper cut-off point below which a candidate cannot win, and this cut-off point is mathematically computed to satisfy required accuracy from a vote result. A result of this will mean many elections will fail to produce a winner. This may seem bad to a public accustomed to having a winner, but this is a proper and good result, and the public needs to be educated why, and that it is or can be very good if public offices remain empty or stop functioning. In my books, I explain why this is the correct result, and that there is a much better system.

Conclusion:

A proper voting system should select the option that best express desired choice. A multi-way vote selection as shown is flawed because it can fail to represent the desired choice. A halt to using such systems is urgently needed, with a proper alternative used. In my other writings, I have shown the requirements of a good voting system, and how to compute a cut-off point.

A Mental Experiment In Guessing: Humans Versus Coin Machines

Intelligence Versus Randomness or Dumbness : Unrepeatable Experiment

If we have a closed room with two groups. One group is made from 100 coin tossing machines. The coins are fair, with YES = 0.5 and therefore they represent Perfect Randomness.

The second group is made from 100 adult humans.

We make a statement and ask if the statement is true, with two reply option: Yes, No. We request only one of the two groups return the answer, but we do not know which group will be answering.

The answer is written on a small glass window as percentage of Yes of the group.

How do we know which group answered?

If the answer returned had a YES near 50%, then it is likely the coin flipping machines answered, or the question was not solvable by the human group (maybe too difficult or its subject is unknown to them).

If YES of the answer was near 100%, then we can say it is much more likely that the answer came from the human group.

A coin machine has zero knowledge and zero intelligence, but it randomly produces 50% correct answers to a question or an exam. So a human being getting 50% correct answers on an exam, or answering questions, or a political candidate receiving 50% support in a poll, or congress getting 50% support on a proposed law is a demonstration of zero knowledge and zero intelligence. We already established that the voting scale begins at 50% and is 0% at that point, now we see that the same applies for correctness or intelligence.

The other related question is: how is getting 51% correctness or support different from 50%. We have learned that there is practically mathematically none.

If we increase the groups size to 10,000 adult humans versus 10000 coin tossing machines, then when YES is near 50%, we can conclude that the answer came from the coin tossing machine or we can conclude that the voters have zero intelligence about the subject of the question. If YES was near 100%, we can conclude that it is likely the voters have perfect intelligence about the issue in the poll.

The implication of these results is critical to understand, because it represents the essence of the voting problem in politics and its mathematics

In politics or law etc. when a poll, a group guess, is talking about a political candidate, a proposed law, a court verdict, often, the poll is done only a single time on the issue involved. Therefore, no matter the answer, the only conclusion we can make is that the answer is likely random or likely intelligent, based on how near it is to 50% or 100%.

Intelligence Versus Randomness or Dumbness: Repeatable But Not Identical Experiment

Next, we look at an experiment where we can ask many questions

The coin machine versus the student

If in the experiment above we put in the room one student and one coin tossing machine.

As an exam to test the student, we ask one hundred exam questions. Only the machine or the student are allowed to answer all of them.

When the answers YES results are delivered, how can you tell if the answers came from the coin tossing machine or the student?

If Yes was near 50%, we can say it likely the coin machine answered or if it was the student, then the student likely does not know his subject.

The implication of these results is critical to understand, because it represents the essence of the problem in grading a test exam and its mathematics.

Next, if we have a chance, to ask more questions, then as the number of questions increase, then we can become more and more sure of the knowledge or ability level of the student. After 1000 or 10000 questions, we can become certain of the results YES and what it implies. If after 10000 questions, the YES of answers is near 50%, then we say the answer came from the coin machine or a student without knowledge or ability. Which puts the student at the same level of knowledge or ability as a coin tossing machine. In short we can say his intelligence in the subject being tested is 0.

If the YES results were near 100%, we can say the answer came from the student and the student has perfect intelligence as it relates to the subject of the exam.

Note: we can see how changing the number of questions (experiment) and the number of people can affect confidence in the results, as per the Group Size Accuracy

Combining the two experiments to establish with confidence the intelligence level of a group

If we modify the first experiment to have 100, 1000, or 10000 questions then we would be able to make with greater confidence how intelligent this group is. For example: looking at 1000 previous votes of congress, we can make a statement about their level of intelligence. Same for looking at the voting history of your countrymen, etc.

Generalization

In politics, law, grading, we face the same situation. When people vote on a candidate to an office, if the YES results are near 50%, and the number of voters is large, we can conclude the voters haze zero intelligence as it relates to the issue in the poll.

In brief: Therefore, a sure 50% YES result is equivalent to a "big zero" intelligence, while a 55% or 65% results etc. are "smaller zeros" until we reach a specific threshold point, as we will find out. This threshold point seems to be when YES is 94% and becomes possibly an acceptable threshold point at 97%. Therefore, the intelligence interval is very narrow, and can roughly be stated to be [0.94, 1].

These conclusions can be very disturbing news to politicians that win office by percentages that do not reflect intelligence in the guess. The intelligence is missing in the candidate, or in the voters, or both. Or if law makers that pass laws with zero intelligence in the poll result, or students that take exams or judges or juries that pass verdicts or company board of directors that decide companies fates, or citizens that decide the fate or life of others in polls.

We can see how randomness (which in important decision-making can be called "stupidity" or error) is maximum when poll results of YES = 50%, and stupidity gets lower and lower to zero when YES = 100% where we have perfect certainty or knowledge, or "intelligence". (Note that YES = 0%, which I ignore, it is opposite of YES = 100% in direction only, pointing left from the 50% center point, but it still conveys intelligence. But it is intelligence in the opposing group. Example: 100% vote in opposition to an issue. The issue fails to get adopted, but in addition, the poll results convey that the opposition group is the intelligent group, not the supporters of the issue, because the results are 100%, but in the opposed direction, which is 0% support. The colors represent stupidity or danger areas, with the red area as greatest stupidity or error area, turning to orange, yellow, green, blue etc. near the graph edge).

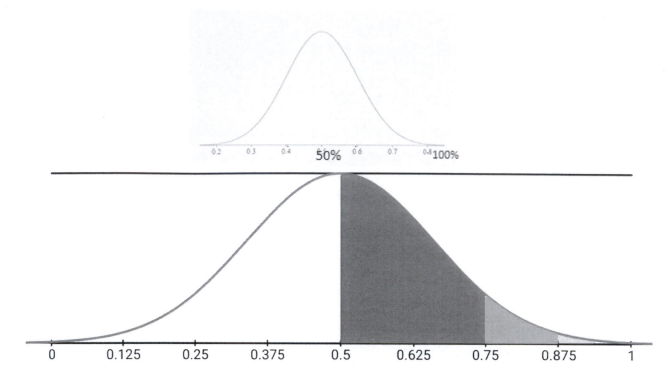

Based on voting proportions distribution, using my formula of YES(YES-NO), for shape of randomness or stupidity when poll results are 50% YES or 0.5, and intelligence calculated as (1 – randomness) distribution curve. The hill is the stupidity graph, the valley is intelligence graph.

A human being performs excellent when he guesses 100% correct in a situation, or specifically in a YES - NO two-sided guess or vote, and is a terrible performer if he guesses 50% correct in a situation, or specifically in a YES - NO two-sided guess or vote.

We can see how intelligence is 0 when poll results of YES are 50%, and gets higher and higher to maximum at YES = 100%. At 100% we have certainty or knowledge, or intelligence.

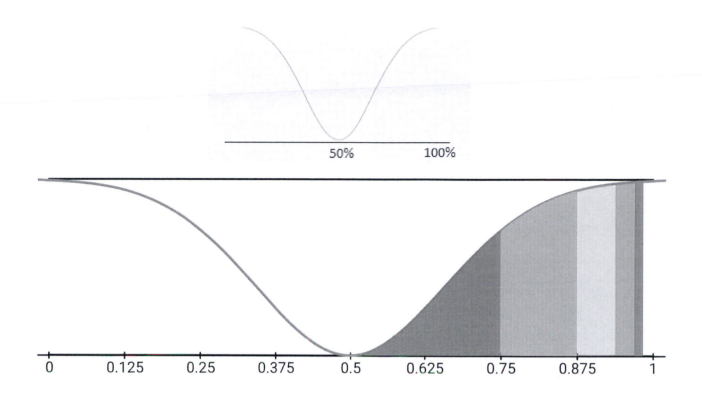

(Read the book A Mathematical Foundation For Politics And Law for exact details).

Ramifications of the experiment

Evaluating a single poll is important. In politics, the results can reflect badly or well on the voters, or the candidate, or both.

And with several polls data, we will have enough data to start being able to isolate if the problem is as a result of the voters intelligence level. If historic data shows poll results to be in the 50% area, we can conclude the voters in total are not intelligent or knowledgeable, because if they were intelligent or knowledgeable, their vote would be unanimous in support or in opposition of the issues. But a result of near 50% says the voters in total are clueless, and if were intelligent in this situation, they would not vote or make a selection, unless a third option is given of 'None Of The Above' but this changes our (Yes, No) choices voting model.

The poll is an instrument we use to measure. It is important that the measuring instrument is accurate and reliable, but it is more important to be able to interpret the results. A poll with 51%, 60%, 70%, 80%, 90%, if a poll was water we drink, implies the water is highly polluted and should not be used or should be rejected to drink or thrown away, and for a poll it implies the results are not trust worthy being polluted by randomness or error or stupidity, and the poll results should not be used and the issue voted in is not adopted, because it failed to meet purity or intelligence threshold standards, which for example may be set to 98% or 99% pollution-free or error-free standard. This is the change that is needed from current practice. It is earth shaking change! The formulas I presented, for the first time, allow the proper calculation and most importantly the proper interpretation of a poll result.

When looking at these simple measuring formulas, we begin to realize the magnitude of the errors produced by the public, governments, and courts etc. in making decisions. The amount of error in decisions is extremely large by scientific standards, as shown in data and graphs elsewhere in this book.

Case 1: The Trial Of Jesus Christ

The event being historically true or not is not important to the analysis. According to some records, a man in the city of Jerusalem, about the year 30 A.D., was accused of criminal acts, reasons not important to the case, and a poll was done among a group of people whether he should be let free from prison or be punished to death. The poll asked the voters if Jesus or another prisoner should be let free. The voters can only select one choice. The voters chose by a voice-call poll to let the other prisoner free. Jesus as a result was executed.

Looking at this poll, we can observe the following:

The poll was unscientific because the results were guessed by a voice call, and not by recording individual voter choices and adding the results.

As a result of such crude method of polling, we can assume that the use or knowledge of formulas to evaluate poll results was not available.

Since this section is about mathematics of politics, consideration of reasons for the criminal accusation, such as freedom of speech and freedom of religion, are not suitable for discussion in this section, until such issues are defined mathematically, such as in the Degrees Of Freedom upcoming section.

Case 2: The Trial Of Socrates

Unlike the case of Jesus, the famous trial of Socrates was documented. It is the only important case in ancient history that is recorded in great detail. As such, and due to the person put on trial, this trial is very important to study.

It happened in Athens, Greece, in the year 399 BCE in what today is regarded by many as the West's foundational culture city, and the city that is regarded as a land of freedom and wisdom. According to some records, there were hints that Athens was considered the regional center for conflict resolution by conflicting parties, who would come from regional areas to settle their problems in its courts or institutions. Socrates was accused of crimes. His trial was judged by jurors who were polled on the verdict decision. They voted that he was guilty, and that he should be killed as punishment.

The number of jury voters seems to have been around 500 with 280 voting Yes, and 220 voted for "a pecuniary fine".

Therefore, the poll results were 280 against 220 jurors for the death penalty. This equates 56% YES to 46% NO, which according to the Poll Accuracy basic formula, produces 10% accuracy, and even lower accuracy is produced when using the more comprehensive accuracy formula that takes Group Size Accuracy into account.

It is noteworthy how unusual the jury size is by today's standard (year 2021). This is an extremely important fact that shows one good aspect of this historic trial. Today's jury sizes may be 10, 20, or 30 people and therefore have inherently an extremely high error rate, not even considering the error rate of a jury of size equal to 1, such as when the poll has a jury of only person judging, as is the case when the case is decided by only one judge. Considering this factor alone, their ancient jury system was better formulaically then today's standard, but still seems full of error, because they did not compute or interpret poll results correctly, and/or did not consider the other factors involved. Jesus, Socrates, Galellio, and millions today continue to suffer bad judgements, and billions of people are led around in politics, law, and culture, by erroneous decisions, because they lack knowledge of voting accuracy calculations.

Degree Of Freedom

Freedom Concept in mathematics

Degree Of Freedom or Degrees Of Freedom is an important concept in mathematics and science. In mechanics, the degree of freedom can be the number of independent motions that are allowed to the body or, in case of a compounded body made of several bodies, it is the number of possible independent relative motions between the pieces. (Wikipedia reference). For example a robot hand that can move in three dimensions has more freedom to move than a hand limited to motion in two dimensions.

In mathematics, it is related to the number of parameters of the system that may vary independently, or the number of dimensions of a system. All this mathematical talk translates to simply: The more choices or options that are available, the higher the degree of freedom is. For example, in probability theory, when tossing a coin that has two sides, and tossing a dice that has six sides, the dice has more landing options, landing choices, (called possibilities) than the coin. So the definition of "Degrees Of Freedom" or "Degree Of Freedom", labelled df or k, is typically defined as equal to $df = k = n - 1$, where n is the number of independent options. Example, a coin with two sides, two landing options, $n = 2$, and its degree of freedom df is $= 2 - 1 = 1$. So the coin has one degree of freedom. If the object has 6 sides, such as a dice, then $n = 6$, and its df is $= 6 - 1 = 5$.

As the choices (the options or possibilities available to the object) increase, its degree of freedom increase. And as these options increase to infinity, df or k increases to infinity. But if the options are only one option, n = 1, this makes df = n - 1 = 0. This means the object has zero degree of freedom. This mathematical notion corresponds almost exactly to the general use of the word "freedom". In life, if you only have 1 option available, it means you have no choice, because it is the only thing available to you. If the food menu in the only available restaurant had only one item, and you must eat immediately in a restaurant or you will die, it means you have no selection choice. Similarly, if you must buy a car, and there is only one car model available, it means you have zero freedom in selection between car models, and must accept this item. In politics, if you have no choice for candidates, or style of government, etc. it means you have no political freedom. In culture, the same applies. But if your options are unlimited, it means your freedom is unlimited.

In probability theory, the possibilities of the object are choices. Also, the sample size of data in an experiment, can add more df. For example: one coin with head, H, and tail, T, sides has H or T options when tossed, n is 2 and df = k = 1, but two coins tossed together have the possibilities of landing {HH, TT, HT, TH}, with n equal to 4 and k equal to 3, or k = 2 if we consider HT and TH to be the same possibility or choice.

Same if the number of tosses for a single coin is 2. Then the possibilities are 4 and k is 3 or 2.

As choices increase, df and k increase, but the probability of a single option landing decreases by 1/n. This can be confusing, but is very good, because as the probability of an option being selected decrease, it mathematically means the resolution or sensitivity is increasing. Having a single noodles choice on the menu may be ok. But having noodles and a choice of spicy noodles on the menu is better for the customer. Even better is having spicy-noodles, medium-spice noodles, light-spice noodles on the menu. More choices, more freedom to choose according to your likings, but now with more choices, the probability of a customer choosing a particular noodle style becomes smaller. Before he had one choice and the restaurant owner new that a customer had 100% probability of choosing non-spicy noodles, because it was the only choice on the menu, and the owner life was simple in preparing food for customers. But with so many choices, the owner has to worry about more preparations, and left over spoiled unbought cooked noodles when there are many choices, since he cannot predict how much customers will buy from each menu choice. It is great for the consumer to have 5, or 10 or 1000 noodle styles on the menu, but it can be a major headache for a restaurant owner to manage. And that is why there are usualy many restaurants instead of just 1. Just like with menu options, having many restaurants, creates higher df, but decreases your chance or probability of selecting a particular restaurant. With only one restaurant in town, the probability of choosing a particular town restaurant is 100%. No choice. For the customer, df or degree of freedom is 0, and the chance or probability of choosing this restaurant is 100%. Not a good situation for the consumer, but an excellent situation for a restaurant owner! But with 100 restaurants in that town, the probability of choosing a particular town restaurant, all things being equal, is 1 out of 100, or 1/100 or 1%. Now, it is a good situation for the customer, where df, or degree of freedom is 99, but for a restaurant owner, the chance of his restaurant being chosen went down from 100% to 1%, which can be a very bad situation for restaurant owners. If the town population is small, there may not be enough customers every day to sustain all 100 restaurants, and competition will be fierce and many of these restaurants may fail. But if the town is big enough to sustain all the restaurants, then the customers will have a good situation and restaurant owners also. What is important to understand is that with more choices, comes more freedom, which comes from freedom of choice, but the probability of selecting a choice becomes smaller, but this is a very positive development. More freedom should produce more choices. More choices produce more accuracy in selection, which produces a higher resolving scale resolution for choice. It is similar to having a measurement ruler with 1 marking, and a measurement ruler with 100 markings. The 100 markings ruler has much higher resolving capability, and thus, much greater measuring accuracy. And better yet, is a scale with 1000 or 1000000 markings, etc.

Therefore, **we can say generally, freedom is highly desirable because it leads to more choices, more choices allow finer selection, wich allows more accuracy in choices, decisions, and therefore more accurate productions. This may be expected to produce a more satisfying life for a human.**

Examples: a painter whose colour pallet includes only 1 possibility of {red}, has n=1, and df or k = 0

A painter with a tool that only has one colour on his palette has n = 1 possibilities to choose from. If the pallet had two colours, then n = 2 and he has more choices but is still very limited. If the palette had {red, blue, yellow, orange, green, violet}, then n = 6 and the painter has more choices to choose from and to create his products. If the number of possibilities also includes combinations of these possibilities, such as mixing of two colours of the pallet, the painter will have even more possibilities that can become almost infinite for choosing a suitable colour. We can see that the number of possibilities is equivalent to the number of available choices. k = n -1 increases as n increases. Therefore "more choices" is equivalent to "more degrees of freedom" or simply more "freedom". This seems logical and translates very well to common language used by non-mathematicians. Same for choosing clothes. Your clothes colours, material, shapes, create more choices or possibilities. Same for a government system types. Or ideas or services. These are all products a human may consume freely. Having a variety of choices in products offers a human being the opportunity to compare and choose according to his desire. Therefore we can see the generalization being abundantly obvious that unlimited Degree Of Freedom for humans provide unlimited possibility space for the production of unlimited options to choose from. Freedom does not guarantee this, but is the best environment for seeing this become a reality.

The following conditions, that are not laws, but are nurtured by an educated culture, are a good environment for adult humans:

1. No harmful interference in the creation of more choices (that is, intentionally limiting choices is harmful).

2. The responsibility is 100% the responsibility of the consumer to limit his personal choices. A government should not use laws to limit risk, as this interferes with the amount of risk a person wants to have in his choices. Some love sky diving, or rock climbing, or big risks in business, or in use of products or experiences, while others hate it as dangerous and should be limited by a government, etc.

3. A person should not interfere to limit the choices of others.

4. It should be presumed that: An adult person knows his own interest better than all others.

5. Having full personal freedom of choice means having **full personal responsibility** for these choices and the consequences of these choices. **Full freedom cannot be established without full personal responsibility**.

6. The choices you make, of good choices or bad choices, when selecting in life are your responsibility. If you delegate this responsibility, giving others power to limit you, you cannot force this delegation of power on others. Delegation of freedom should not be forced, it is always a personal choice. If you want to delegate your freedom to a government, you are free to do so, and this government can govern you, but this same government should not be able to govern a human that does not delegate his freedom to it. If you want a government, impose it on your self only, and not coercively on others who do not want it.

Therefore, by the formulas presented, we can see that freedom is the best choice for human beings. And conversely, this also can lead to the conclusion that any law is a limit on human freedom.

 If this is not abundantly obvious to uneducated human beings in this mathematics or to politicians who are not educated in this mathematics, it seems that before a politician or person feels motivated to interfere in the affairs of humans, at the very minimum he should be aware of this mathematics .

Human freedom is now founded on a solid mathematical foundation.

Freedom, which is properly defined as Freedom Of Choice, and accuracy, both increase with more choice, and are therefore directly proportional to the mathematically defined Degree Of Freedom.

This can serve as a mathematical proof that Freedom Of Choice is a mathematically optimum environment for humans.

Freedom Of Choice is now a mathematically defined term.

Formula: Human Freedom is equivalent to the mathematical Degree Of Freedom definition,
and is directly proportional to the amount of available choices

---

Exercise for mathematicians: Is it proper for mathematicians to petition governments if their mistakes are mathematical and extremely serious in consequences? Is this a mathematics issue or a social issue?

The Threat Index

The Threat Index is an index I developed as a tool that can be used to measure or classify individuals or groups potential threat level to other human beings.

The Threat Index to other humans is defined as inversely proportional to the lack of knowledge of a human or a group about freedom mathematics, or the conclusions of freedom mathematics.

Threat level $\propto 1 /$ [(knowledge of freedom mathematics, OR knowing similar conclusions) AND (accepting them AND practicing them)]

Opposition to freedom

There are those that oppose freedom as a political standard, for their own personal or group reasons.

Regarding the pressures that come from those opposing human freedom. A natural question comes to mind: How can they oppose it if it is mathematically correct? Are they either uneducated in the subject, or have the knowledge but intent to harm human beings?

If they are uneducated, there seems to be self interest in spreading knowledge about the political, cultural, and economic effects of freedom, and specifically, the very simple Poll Accuracy equations. If they know of the mathematical results as accurate and reject them, I cannot discuss this in this book further, as beyond scope at this time. But worth noting that many times in history, people took to guns or severed historic connections to other people, when their freedom was limited or properties confiscated involuntarily.

Here are graphs of k = Degree Of Freedom (number of choices) as k increases. K' is the rate of change of k, called its derivate. With magnified portions of the graph.

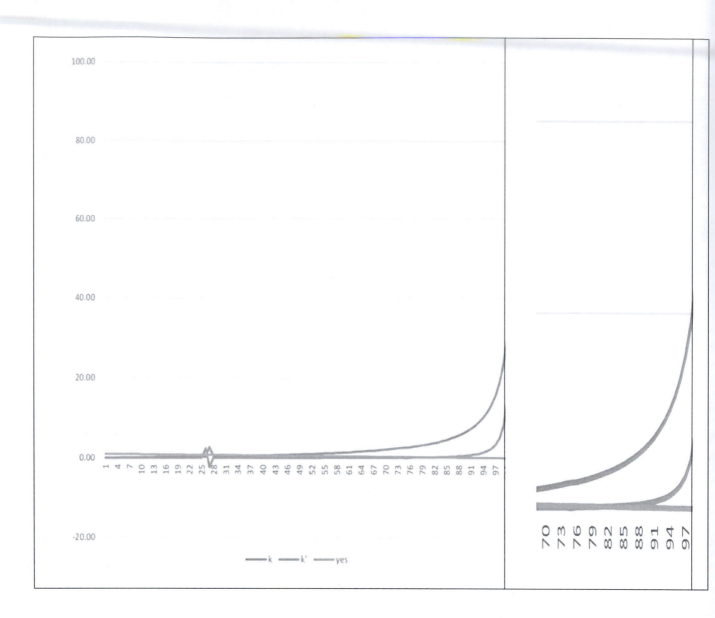

The above two graphs for n = number of possibilities or choices, k = Degree Of Freedom = n - 1, and k' = derivative of k (rate of change in k), and YES.

It is important to note that the Degree Of Freedom (freedom) remains very low, until we reach near the level of 94% YES at which point it starts to increase.

General notes:

Summary: As N increases, k increases, but inadequately, until we reach the threshold point of around 97%, at which point, the degree of freedom starts to increase materially, and the measuring scale precision begins to be high enough to allow greater accuracy in calculations and helps to lower chance of error. In short, a minimum of 97% YES seems to be needed if we want to explore in accuracy and freedom, and to limit threats and harm from errors.

Academic Future Project For Increasing Human Intelligence

Law is usually the creation of law makers, who are usually the product of politics, and politics is usually the product of culture. At the heart of a culture is communication between individuals. Communication is done through language usually. Language is generally composed of words and rules for using them called grammar. Language is also a foundation for thinking. Therefore, a good language is an essential tool for good thinking. The better the language is, the better the thinking should be. Therefore, it seems that a good language should be mathematically consistent since mathematics is the most rigorous form of logic we have. Therefore, it is important that human languages have an explicitly defined underlying mathematical structure that is self-consistent. This creates a logical language, that is absorbed from childhood, as any other language, except that it adds great logical ability to all children, without much effort or schooling. If the culture uses such a language, almost every child, by the time they mature, will absorb an enormous amount of logic and knowledge that is essential for proper thinking ability. Therefore, this seems to be one of the greatest gifts a parent can give a child, for their benefits and equally important for ours. With schooling or without, you can ensure a minimal level of thinking ability, that protects us from harms of those with poor thinking ability and the damage such individuals do to others, and the other consequences of others trying to build politics and laws to coercively protect themselves from such ignorance. Another problem is that even those who think of themselves to be educated can be equally uneducated in important areas, and they do equal amount of damage to others by their actions, no matter how good their intentions may be.

Therefore, one of the most important projects humans can undertake is the remolding of their existing languages to have a mathematical defined foundation, by building a proper dictionary and proper grammar. They can start from the most important words, usually these are used often in mathematics, and moving downward to physics, and downward to other sciences with the hierarchy defined by how well scientifically defined the subject already is. For example, the first project would be the creation of a "Mathematical Dictionary Of Language". Example: Starting with Binomial Theory, its language is close to common use language. This is one essential criteria, that will also force mathematicians to change some of their terms, to match common language. While probability theory language uses the terms "probability p" and "its compliment q" , where the general public often does not understand the word "probability" mathematically, and does not know what a "compliment" means in mathematical terms, Binomial Theory uses the words "Success" and "Failure", which the general public can immediately grasp and relate to from common experience. So spending months or years to make a child or adult understand the words "Probability and its compliment" becomes a task that can be accomplished maybe in hours or less. Most importantly, the general public can carry their personal experience in daily life to this new understanding, and they will naturally remember it for life without much effort, while they are likely to not remember the other words if they do not practice mathematics as part of their daily life. So talking about Success and Failure and teaching them that the basic probability equation can be defined as "Success percentage plus Failure percentage must equal 1", becomes much easier to explain. Now we have to do the same for the word "percentage" and to define it in the dictionary in similar easy terms. So the dictionary would have:

Success Definition: An event you think is a success. Example: If you think getting educated is a success, then you have succeeded in this area. If not, then a person failed. Or when talking to a potential customer, if you convince them to buy your cookies, it is a Success, Otherwise it is a Failure. etc.

Failure Definition: Opposite Of Success, or Not Success

Not Definition: Opposite. Or opposite in direction. Example: blah blah blah

Error Definition: Distance of a result from the target …

Accuracy = 100 percent minus error percentage …

Square Root definition: Erasing this term from mathematics textbooks may be very wise, accept keeping it as a historic term, and replacing it with "square side" or "Side of a square". My guess is that few in the general public know what a square root is or know how to compute it, but simply changing its name to "square side", it may take minutes instead of weeks, or months or years to teach and remember this term for life. Most people know what a square is, or can learn it easily, and will easily learn what the side of a square is and how to compute it, given an area of a square. The square area is 16, how much is the square side?

Next, we have to define the word "area", etc.

By the time you are finished creating this dictionary, and hopefully as a group effort, per the great work that created WIKIPEDIA, then when children learn about words, and absorb grammar naturally in their interaction growing with parents and others, we can be sure that their thinking has an underlying sound logical structure. I can think of few things that improve human intelligence as this project.

(Side note: Wikipedia, the free internet encyclopedia, was founded by: Larry Sanger (born 1968), American internet project developer, and Jimmy Wales (born 1966), American-British internet entrepreneur).

If this dictionary is done for one language, it can be easily translated to other languages, and other languages can add maybe their own advantages to this dictionary. Different languages have in them variations that can be superior to other languages, and this becomes shared, if they want to share it.

Even more important why this project is a necessity or will be, is because computers' computing ability is increasing at enormous rate. Just like there were no electronic computers few years ago, and all of sudden, they were invented , and their rate of ability grew exponentially, this is likely to continue, and another quantum jump in ability is likely to occur, that will take computing ability far beyond, and similarly with the creation of new robots. Today, a mere $20 cell phone with a good chess program can easily beat almost any chess player on earth. Chess is supposed to be a human domain of intelligence, and we can see it is not, or that it can be automated. The same can happen in other areas, with humans becoming more and more like idiots compared to these machines. Even though we are creating the computer and the programs that run it, we find ourselves unable to beat our own creation! And when a closed loop is formed, of computers by themselves designing other computers, we will have a bigger problem. The only way for us to stay in this loop is if our language is mathematically perfectly correct or self-consistent. Even having one error in it can be disastrous, as a defect in a computer language, or a single defective transistor. Ways are found to deal with such issues, but the heart of the problem should be understood. Therefore, soon, we may be communicating with computers at a deep level. Currently, it happens, but is extremely superficial in power, even when useful. In the future, when you talk to a computer as to any other lay person about a difficult engineering problem or any problem in life, the computer may generate a set of equations composed of one million complex mathematical equations, and solve your problem in few seconds or instantly. This will be an enormous empowerment of human ability, but if your language is not mathematical at its root, you will have problems communicating with such advanced computers, and you will be left behind. It is like having a wrist watch that is too small to have a keyboard, or even a screen, and has only spoken language as input. If you cannot speak because of a physical speech problem, you cannot take advantage of it, and more importantly for the future, even if you can speak to it, you need to speak to it in a sound language.

I mention this issue here for academics to understand this problem and start working on it. It relates to having an intelligent human being, and this seems like an important issue with ramifications in many social areas, including freedom and peace. A person that is not self-consistent in mind and body, is a weaker person than his/her optimum (best), and can be vulnerable to harm from others, and can unknowingly cause great harm to others.

Academic Project About Stability And Sustainability Of Freedom

A very important issue that should be solved mathematically is: Given that the uneducated at this time far outnumber the educated, what is the best strategy to protect freedom of choice from mob rule? And legalized thievery using confiscatory tax laws. The history of men kind has been a record of utter failure in this regard. The real or fictional character Robin Hood is said to be a thief that stole from innocent rich people, but is a hero to many who care less that he was stealing from innocent people, as long as he gave them the money. Many law makers are much bigger thieves, and are proud of it, and are loved by those receiving the stolen money.

At what point does freedom come into stable equilibrium and become a self-sustaining system? This is a question that must be answered mathematically. Unstable equilibrium is a ball on top of a hill (a downward facing parabola) and is unstable because we cannot predict its final position when disturbed, and stable equilibrium is a ball inside a curved bottom glass (a upward facing parabola), where we can predict its final position even when disturbed.

If the 9 families in the town of F.O. overpowered the single family by use of law, to put them under their rule and control, and try to confiscate their money and property, then, are there solutions to this question compatible with freedom? I leave it to others to explore this extremely important and central question.

It is difficult to explain the evolution of a free social system versus a planned, and pre-programmed social system to an uneducated human. A new born animal, such as a Gazel, minutes after birth, is able to run and outpace a new born human who needs about one year, two years or more to walk or run stably. A planned social system is similar in that it far surpasses a slow and free evolving system at the beginning of its development. Yet, years later, when this child matures, he far outpaces any animal in ability and intelligence. The Gazel may still be able to outrun him, but he can easily catch it using intelligence. The human is a million times more intelligent maybe, but needs much more time and energy to develop and mature. And the payoff in such investment seems worthwhile. Same for a planned social system versus a freedom-of-choice system, you need patience and intelligence raising it, and the good fruits will hopefully come in due time. Human history is a record of utter failure in terms of the widespread availability of freedom of choice.

Some mathematics for those who know it, or the curious, from the book A Mathematical Foundation For Politics And Law:

The Simple Majority Voting System Has 0% Guaranteed Accuracy

A Simple Majority Voting system is where a poll is allowed to be adopted by having 50% of the voters + 1 voter, voting in support in a poll.

The guaranteed maximum accuracy of a Simple Majority Voting system is 0%. That is, this system has no guarantee of accuracy. Proof:

The vote accuracy equation, which is historic in that for the first time in recorded history, we can measure the accuracy of a vote mathematically, is Accuracy = YES - NO - 2 x GMOE = (2 x YES) - 2 x GMOE ; GMOE is the statistical MARGIN OF ERROR = Z x Standard Error

If YES = 50% + 1/n, is sufficient for poll adoption, with n = total number of voters

NO = 50% - 1/n

Accuracy = 2/n - 2 x GMOE = $\dfrac{2}{n} - \dfrac{4}{\sqrt{n}}$

If n is maximum and equals infinity, $Accuracy = \dfrac{2}{\infty} - \dfrac{4}{\sqrt{\infty}} = 0 - 0 = 0 = 0\%$

For a given YES greater or equal to 0.5, we have seen that the accuracy function increases monotonically with n.

Therefore, the guaranteed maximum accuracy of a Simple Majority Voting system is 0%.

Consensus System: This is a Unanimous Voting System. Advantages: For any group size, it offers the maximum voting accuracy possible.

Proof: Since Poll Accuracy is a function of YES and Group size, as the Accuracy equation above shows, and is monotonically increasing for both variables, YES is always 1 or 100% for a unanimous vote, which is the maximum YES, for any group size, which therefore produces the maximum poll accuracy possible.

A Consensus System is a complete Freedom System, because a group cannot do anything against the will of any individual, since the individual in effect, has veto power. This proves that a complete Freedom

System has maximum accuracy and therefore is optimum when compared to other systems! Now this is beautiful human related mathematics!!!!!!!

Storming the castle syndrome

Much is done in human behaviour from fear. The standard for some is "do no wrong" . If it is wrong to attack innocent people to steal their property, no matter how rich they are, and how poor you are, then it is also wrong to "impose" taxes on others forcefully, by gun or by law or by deception etc. Many innocent people all over the world are subject to this fear of "storm the castle" or "storm the house" or "storm the person walking on the street", and, to appease these evil attackers, or potential attackers, before they start the attack, innocent people feel "obliged to give money, or food, or property, to appease evil". That is not a good state for humans to be in, or a good standard for humans to uphold.

But if a human being knows proper behaviour and improper behaviour, according to the standard mentioned above, then some, hungry, and desiring objects that do not belong to them, may intentionally, make themselves stupid, in order to gain courage or ability to attack the castle. So if they have intelligence in them, some intelligent humans or beings reach out to their mind, as you reach with your hand to a box, and remove intelligence from it, knowing that if they keep this intelligence, they cannot storm the castle, or steal what belongs to others. So knowingly, some humans or beings, reach to their mind, and throw away intelligence, either because other forces is making them, or because they see intelligence as a disadvantage in some situations. If we value intelligence, the subtraction of intelligence is improper behaviour. If you think it is proper, or intelligent behaviour to subtract from your intelligence so you can attack me, do not be upset if I subtract from your intelligence.

I presented many ideas, including mathematics. Objects in life can be very costly depending on their value. And, to take what is not your is not proper behaviour. If you use these ideas and mathematics improperly, there is a cost for them, now and in the afterlife that you know. And if you use them properly, remember the cost already paid.

A Vote Result Calculator Example:

Simply copy this JavaScript computer code bellow and paste into a blank file, and name the file votecalculator.html, html file name extension is important. And open the file in a browser and use to experiment or modify:

```
<html>

<head>

  <meta name="viewport" content="width=device-width"  initial-scale="1">

  <script src='file:///android_asset/app.js'></script>

</head>




<Script>

//Called when application is started.

function OnStart()

{

}

</Script>




<script>

  //Called after application is started.

  function ShowDocumentation()

  {


  }

</script>




<body onload="app.Start()">




<style>


    body {

 background-color: white;
```

```css
  margin:10;
}

.navbar {
  overflow: hidden;
  background-color: #333;
  position: fixed;
  top: 0;
  width: 100%;
}

.navbar a {
  float: center;
  display: block;
  color: #f2f2f2;
  text-align: center;
  padding: 14px 16px;
  text-decoration: none;
  font-size: 17px;
}

.navbar a:hover {
  background: #ddd;
  color: black;
}

.navbar img {
  float: left;
  display: block;
  color: #f2f2f2;
  text-align: center;
  padding: 14px 16px;
  text-decoration: none;
  font-size: 17px;
}
```

```css
.navbar img:hover {
  background: #ddd;
  color: black;
}

.main {
  padding: 16px;
  margin-top: 110px;
  /* height: 1500px; /* Used in this example to enable scrolling */
}

label {
  color: gray
  text-align: center;
}

input {
  color: blue;
  text-align: center;
  bold;
  border:solid 2px blue;
  margin: 5px 5px;
  outline:solid 5px lightblue;
}

select {
  color: blue;
  text-align: center;
  bold;
  border:solid 2px blue;
  margin: 5px 5px;
  outline:solid 5px lightblue;
}

button {
  color: blue;
  text-align: center;
```

```css
    bold;
    border:solid 2px blue;
     margin: 5px 5px;
     outline:solid 5px lightblue;

}


span {
color: red;
 text-align: center;
}


h1 {
 color: blue;
   text-align: center;
 bold;
 border:solid 2px blue;
   margin: 5px 5px;
    outline:solid 5px lightblue;
     background-color: white
}




h4 {
 color: gray;
   text-align: center;
 bold;
 border:solid 1px blue;
   margin: 5px 5px;
    outline:solid 1px lightblue;
     background-color: white;
}




</style>
```

```html
<div class="navbar">

<a href=""><h1>Vote Result Calculator</h1></a>

<a href=""><h4>Accuracy & Error Of A Vote</h4></a>



</div>


<div class="main">

</div>



<br/>

<br/>

<b>

        Vote Input:<br/>

<label for="YESVoters">Number Of Voters In Favor Or Yes: </label>

<input id="YESVoters" name="YESVoters" type="number" min="1" step="1"  placeholder="number voting YES" maxlength="10" required autofocus> </input><br/><br/>

<label for="NOVoters">Number Of Voters Opposed Or No: </label>

<input id="NOVoters" name="NOVoters" type="number" min="0" step="1"  placeholder="number voting NO" maxlength="10" required> </input> <br/><br/>


<label for="ChoiceSystem">Are the voter selection choices {Yes , No} or {Yes , No, Dont Know}, etc. : </label>

 <select name="ChoiceSystem" id="ChoiceSystem">

  <option value="2">{Yes , No} </option>

  <option value="3">{Yes , Dont Know, NO} </option>

  <option value="5">{Yes , Likely Yes, Dont Know, Likely No, No} </option>

   <option value="7">{Yes , Likely Yes, Maybe Yes, Dont Know, Maybe No, Likely No, No} </option>

 </select>

 <br><br>


<label for="Z">Choose a Confidence Level in the calculated results, such 95%, 99.73% or 99.99% :</label>

 <select name="Z" id="Z">

  <option value="2">95.44%</option>

  <option value="3">99.73%</option>

  <option value="4">99.99%</option>

 </select>

 <br><br>
```

```
</b>

<br/>

<button onclick="calc()">

Calculate

</button>

<br/>

<br/>

Total Voters = <span id="TotalVoters"></span><br/>

Vote Net In Favor = <span id="VoteResult"></span>% <br/>

<b>

Vote Accuracy = <span id="VoteAccuracy"></span>% <br/>

Vote Error = <span id="VoteError"></span>%<br/>


 <span id="NegativeVoteAccuracyMessage"></span> <br/>


</b>
```

A basic vote announcement would be as follows: `<br/>`

`<b>` The Vote Accuracy or The Vote Quality is `<span id="VoteAccuracy1"></span>% </b>`.

`<br/><br/>`

Additionally, an announcement can add "this means the Vote Error is" `<span id="VoteError1"></span>% <br/>`

Using the statistical measure "Confidence Level" in a public announcement can be extremely confusing to the public, since this can be easily confused with Accuracy. This measure nonetheless should be recorded with the vote and accounted for as it is a critical part of the result.

As for voting in general, it is important that an organization set a prespecified "Accuracy Threshold" that must be achieved by the vote, for the vote to be adopted. Example: A vote must have no less than 98% Accuracy Threshold, which alternatively means, the organization will not tolerate more than 2% error rate.

The public in general has no understanding of the concept of error in a vote or a poll. Therefore, it is important that they are educated or made acquainted with the concept. Here are very detailed explanations of the accuracy equation made simple:

```
</br>

</br>

<center>

Opposed voters   <b><--------      --------></b>   In Favor voters<br/>

 <span id="NoVotersVector"></span>   or  <span id="No"></span>%   <b><--------      --------></b>   <span
id="YesVotersVector"></span>  or  <span id="Yes"></span>%


<br/>
```

=

 % Net In Favor

　　　READ THIS BELLOW AND SCROLL DOWN

　　　| | | | | | | | | | | | | | | | | | | | | | | | | |

Opposed means opposite direction. If a single In Favor voter has a weight or power equal to 1, it means a single Opposed Voter has a weight or power equal to 1 in the opposite direction which is represented as -1

Now you know the first principle in voting calculations:

 A voter weight is NOT a number, but is a vector

A vector is something that has a magnitude and direction, such as:

In Favor voter vector is   -------->   = 1

Opposed voter vector is   <--------   = -1

Now the second principle in voting calculations:

 A vote has two parts: The In Favor part, and the Opposed part. A Vote Result is the sum of both parts.

Therefore, when you add voters, you are adding vectors, NOT numbers, and adding vectors looks like "A Rope Pulling Contest" :

Opposed voters   <--------   -------->   In Favor voters

   <--------   -------->

　=

```
<br/>
```

`<span id="VoteTotal"></span> Net Voters In Favor<br/>`

`</center>`

`<!-- infavor must be positive integer and greater than opposed-->`

`<br/>`

In percentages, the numbers are:

`<br/>`

Opposed `<span id="No1"></span>`%

`<------- -------->`

`<span id="Yes1"></span>`% In Favor

`<br/>`

`=`

`<br/>`

Vote Result = `<span id="VoteResult3"></span>`% Net In Favor

`</br>`

`</center>`

`</br>`

Group Size Error or in statistics the effect of Sample Size on error, is the third component in voting, and it is the error that is purely the result of the group size, and does not depend on how a group votes; For example: A group of size 1 person, or 3 persons or 10 person has very high error or low credibility, while a vote by 1000 persons has less error or higher credibility, and a vote with 100,000 voters is much better to ensure vote results are credible. Low credibility implies high error in a vote.

The total Group Size Error is defined as 2 * Margin Of Error of the probability p = 1/N, where the number of answer choices N = `<span id="ChoiceSystem1"></span>` is the number of choices available to answer the poll question, where Z is the statistical Z-Score, and the Voter Guess probability = 1/N = `<span id="GuessProbability"></span>` is based on the choices system the voter is allowed, be it {Yes , No} or {Yes , No , Don't Know}, etc. Note the principle that the important voting principle that "The more choices are provided to a voter for an answer, the greater the poll accuracy will be. Example: 3 choices {Yes , Don't Know, No} provide greater poll accuracy than the 2 choices {Yes , No}".

In this case, the total number of voters n produces a Group Size Error that is equal to `<span id="SampleError"></span>`%

`</br>`

`</br>`

poll results Total Margin Of Error is defined as Z * 2 * sqrt((YES x NO)/n), where Z is the statistical Z-Score, YES & NO are poll means of yes voters and no voters.

In this case, the total number of voters n produces a poll Total MOE that is equal to `<span id="PollMOE"></span>`%

`</br>`

`</br>`

Therefore in voting, an important principle is: "A bigger group of voters produces more credibility or reliability or accuracy and less error in a vote all other things being equal, and therefore, the Group Size Error will be smaller when the number of voters participating in a vote is bigger."

</br>

 It is important to compute the needed group size for a desired minimal accuracy. A group of 1, 5, 10, or 50 may be extremely insufficient for high accuracy decisions based on a vote. Experiment with the calculator by putting different numbers, to see the effect and learn how much error a specific group size adds to a vote.

</br>

The second factor in vote accuracy is: Just like gun target shooting, when you hit the target, your accuracy is high. And the further away from the target you hit, the less accuracy you have. Same for a vote or a poll. With a vote, the target is 100% success. This is maximum accuracy, and the further away the vote support is, the less accuracy you have.

</br>

Therefore, a critical principle in voting is "a vote that gets 60% support has very poor accuracy compared to a vote that gets 80% support, which in turn has very poor accuracy compared to a vote that gets 95% support. You get the point I hope."

Therefore, the net support = percent of Yes voters minus percent of No voters , computes this factor.

 Experiment with numbers, and you will learn a very simple and important equation for accuracy in voting and in general.

</br>

</br>

The Vote Accuracy equation = (Yes% - No%) - Group size Error% - Poll MOE = % - % - % = %

</br>

The Vote Error = %

</br>

        Looking at a Vote Error, every 1% error rate in a vote can have extremely serious consequences:</br>

Example 1: A 1% error rate in court jury verdicts means that one person is convicted falsely for every 100 trials.</br>

 Therefore, a 20% error rate implies 20 persons are convicted falsely by the courts for every 100 trials. Therefore, if the court system has 10,000 trials yearly, the courts are convicting 20 x 100 = 2000 persons falsely. To compute the number of people injured by an error rate, multiply the error rate by the affected population.</br>

 </br>

 Example 2: A 1% error in a parliament or congress vote or decision means that one person is injured by the adopted law or decision for every 100 persons.</br>

 But, a country or a state or a city usually has a much larger population than 100. If the country's population for example is 10 million persons, this implies 100000 persons are injured by the parliament or congress when adopting the new law or decision. But this is for only 1% error rate. What if the vote had 20% error rate? The number of those innocently injured will be 20 x 100000 = 2 million people! There are more considerations that can be included in the calculations.</br>

 Same for a corporate board vote, or a committee vote, etc.

 </br>

Injury, damage, or risk, may be general terms that are associated with error. The injury can be a wide range of types: Physical as in a wrongful death sentence or imprisonment or confinement, or wrongful financial assessment, or increasing risk to a person to all these factors by a law or a decision, that are the result of a vote, or a as some call it 'a poll'.

To compute the number of people injured from vote error, enter the population size the vote encompasses:

<label for="PopulationSize">Population Size: </label>

<input id="PopulationSize" name="PopulationSize" type="number" min="1" step="1" placeholder="Population Size" maxlength="10" required autofocus> </input>

The number of injured people due to this error rate is:

<button onclick="calc()">

Calculate

</button>

<label for="CostOfErrorToSinglePerson">Input Cost Of Error To A Single Person.

If the cost is not in money units, convert the cost to money units.

Examples: 1. If the cost is the life of a person, then you may look at the actuarial cost of a life as computed by insurance companies.

This life loss cost in the U.S.A. may be $1 million, while in Mexico it may be $200,000.

If the cost is prison confinenment, then one factor in calculating the cost is the number of days in jail, and how much money im wages this person lost based on his salary.

Another loss this person may suffer is harm to his reputation, emotional and psychological harms from not being in comfort with family and friends and relaxation.

Another factor he may suffer is harm from other inmates, etc.

Many of these harms may be irreversable and a money cost may not be possible to calculate or the cost may be infinite.

Try your best to create money cost equivalents to the different types of costs.

Another kind of cost is direct cost of financial cost such as caused by a new tax law, or a court verdict, etc.</label>

<input id="CostOfErrorToSinglePerson" name="CostOfErrorToSinglePerson" type="number" min="1" step="1" placeholder="Cost Of Single Error" maxlength="10" required autofocus> </input>

The total cost of errror or Vote Error Cost in money units is:

<button onclick="calc()">

Calculate

</button>

TotalCostOfError

</br>

</br>

</br>

<p>

Warning: Use of this calculator is at your own risk. Consult a professional mathematician (expert in probability AND statistics) for important validations.

</br>

</br>

Reference: The book "A Mathematical Foundation For Politics And Law" by Jamil Kazoun

</br>

The name Vote Result Calculator™ is a trademark of Jamil Kazoun

</br>

The mathematics formulas were developed by Jamil Kazoun as per the provided book reference.

</br>

Use of these is permitted providing proper attribution is given.

</br>

</p>

```
<script>
function inPercent(n) {
 var r = 100 * n ;
 return r.toFixed(2) ;
 }


function calc() {
var YESVoters = document.getElementById('YESVoters').value || 0;
var NOVoters = document.getElementById('NOVoters').value || 0;
var  PopulationSize = document.getElementById('PopulationSize').value || 0;


var YESVoters = parseInt(YESVoters, 10);
var NOVoters = parseInt(NOVoters, 10);
var YesVotersVector = YESVoters ;
var NoVotersVector = NOVoters * (-1) ;
var VoteTotal = YESVoters - NOVoters ;


 var TotalVoters = YESVoters + NOVoters;
 var Yes = (YESVoters / TotalVoters) ;
 var No = (NOVoters / TotalVoters) ;


 var VoteResult = Yes - No ;
```

```javascript
var Z = document.getElementById('Z').value || 2;

var ConfidenceLevelText = "";

var ChoiceSystem = document.getElementById('ChoiceSystem').value || 2;

var GuessProbability = 0.5;


if (Z == 2) {ConfidenceLevelText = "95.44";}

else if (Z == 3) {ConfidenceLevelText = "99.73";}

else if (Z == 4) {ConfidenceLevelText = "99.99";}

else  {ConfidenceLevelText = "error!!";

}


if (ChoiceSystem == 2) {GuessProbability = 1/2;}

else if (ChoiceSystem == 3) {GuessProbability = 1/3;}

else if (ChoiceSystem == 5) {GuessProbability = 1/5;}

 else if (ChoiceSystem == 7) {GuessProbability = 1/7;}

else  {GuessProbability = "error!!";

}


var PollMOE=  Z*2*Math.sqrt((Yes*(1 - Yes))/ TotalVoters);


 var SampleError =  Z*2*Math.sqrt((GuessProbability*(1 - GuessProbability))/ TotalVoters);

 var VoteAccuracy = VoteResult -  SampleError - PollMOE ;

 var VoteError = 1 - VoteAccuracy ;


if(YESVoters <= 0) {alert('Please enter a positive number of those voting In Favor or Yes'); return;}

    if(NOVoters < 0) {alert('Please enter 0 or a positive number of those voting Opposed or No'); return;}

       if(YESVoters < NOVoters) {alert('The number of those voting In Favor or Yes should be greater or equal to those opposed. If not, flip
the vote question, and place No voters in Yes box, and Yes voters in the No box'); return;}


InjuredPopulation = Math. ceil(VoteError*PopulationSize)


      if(PopulationSize < 0) {alert('Please enter 0 or a positive number for population size'); return;}

      if(PopulationSize < InjuredPopulation) {InjuredPopulation = PopulationSize;} // the error rate is greater than 100 percent

      if( InjuredPopulation < 0 ) {InjuredPopulation = PopulationSize;} // we have negative accuracy, or erro greater than 100 percent


      var NegativeVoteAccuracyMessage = '';
```

```javascript
    if (VoteAccuracy < 0) {NegativeVoteAccuracyMessage = 'A negative Vote Accuracy occurs when the number of people participating
in a vote is too low, which generates a large error. To experiment, increase the number of voters. The second factor is that the percent of
Yes voters may be  too low.   Typically a Yes vote of less than 75% has high error.  Read the explanations further down the page for greater
understanding.';}


var CostOfErrorToSinglePerson =  document.getElementById('CostOfErrorToSinglePerson').value || 0;


if(CostOfErrorToSinglePerson < 0) {alert('Please enter 0 or a positive number for The Cost Of A Single Error to a single person'); return;}


  var TotalCostOfError = CostOfErrorToSinglePerson*InjuredPopulation;


document.getElementById('TotalCostOfError').innerText = TotalCostOfError ;

document.getElementById('YesVotersVector').innerText = YesVotersVector ;

document.getElementById('NoVotersVector').innerText = NoVotersVector ;

document.getElementById('TotalVoters').innerText = TotalVoters ;

document.getElementById('VoteTotal').innerText = VoteTotal ;

document.getElementById('Yes').innerText = inPercent(Yes);

document.getElementById('No').innerText = inPercent(No);

document.getElementById('VoteResult').innerText = inPercent(VoteResult);

document.getElementById('SampleError').innerText = inPercent(SampleError);

document.getElementById('VoteAccuracy').innerText = inPercent(VoteAccuracy);

document.getElementById('VoteError').innerText = inPercent(VoteError);

document.getElementById('GuessProbability').innerText = GuessProbability;




// document.getElementById('VoteResult1').innerText = inPercent(VoteResult);

document.getElementById('VoteResult2').innerText = inPercent(VoteResult);

document.getElementById('VoteResult3').innerText = inPercent(VoteResult);

document.getElementById('VoteResult4').innerText = inPercent(VoteResult);

document.getElementById('VoteAccuracy1').innerText = inPercent(VoteAccuracy);

document.getElementById('VoteAccuracy2').innerText = inPercent(VoteAccuracy);

document.getElementById('VoteError1').innerText = inPercent(VoteError);

document.getElementById('VoteError2').innerText = inPercent(VoteError);

document.getElementById('SampleError1').innerText = inPercent(SampleError);

document.getElementById('NegativeVoteAccuracyMessage').innerText = NegativeVoteAccuracyMessage;

document.getElementById('InjuredPopulation').innerText = InjuredPopulation;

document.getElementById('ChoiceSystem1').innerText = ChoiceSystem;
```

```
document.getElementById('YesVotersVector1').innerText = YesVotersVector ;

document.getElementById('NoVotersVector1').innerText = NoVotersVector ;

document.getElementById('Yes1').innerText = inPercent(Yes);

document.getElementById('No1').innerText = inPercent(No);

document.getElementById('PollMOE').innerText = inPercent(PollMOE);

document.getElementById('PollMOE2').innerText = inPercent(PollMOE);




    }


// extra scripts such as for pop up dialog for documentation etc.


</script>


</body>

</html>
```

End of software code.

This Book Is About Freedom

This book about freedom can be EXTREMELY THREATENING to **many** governments or INDIVIDUALS or OFFICIALS and other political and social groups.

Many oppressive governments, cultures, and individuals or in many modern and rich and powerful governments and countries the individuals in them have interests that put them in opposition to freedom (freedom of choice). The one thing you should understand is that I am only one private citizen, facing great pressures and threats that are uninvited. I have been attacked many times before, and my life has been made extremely difficult and dangerous. They simply see my writings and speech as a major threat. My situation has become very difficult because of this and other issues I face. If you feel these writings are greatly needed values, then help! Just make sure you have straight hair, and you are not a Muslim or a Jew, because that is a personal issue as to who I want help from, and only if you agree with the book, then send badly needed donations to my PayPal account: JamilKazoun@gmail.com.